A Dash of Elegance

A Dash of
Elegance

CHARLES G. REAVIS

Photography by Tony Cenicola

MACMILLAN·USA

MACMILLAN
A Prentice Hall Macmillan Company
15 Columbus Circle
New York, NY 10023

MACMILLAN is a registered trademark of Macmillan, Inc.
All food styling by Roscoe Betsill, except on page 98.

Library of Congress Cataloging-in-Publication Data
Reavis, Charles, 1948–
    A dash of elegance / Charles G. Reavis : photography by Tony Cenicola.
      p.   cm.
    Includes index.
    ISBN 0-02-601210-3
    1. Cookery (Vinegar)   2. Oils and fats, Edible.   3. Sherry.
I. Title.
TX819.V5R43   1994   94-3032
641.6'22—dc20   CIP

Photography prop credits: Page 72, plates from Fishs Eddy and table from ABC Carpet
& Home; page 78, plate from Fishs Eddy; page 92, plate from Platypus and cupboard
from ABC Carpet & Home; page 100, bowl from Fishs Eddy; page 102, plate from
Platypus and table, candles, and cupboard from ABC Carpet & Home; page 108, dishes and table from ABC Carpet & Home; page 112, plates and table from ABC Carpet
& Home; page 116, plate from Platypus; page 120, plates from Platypus; page 128,
plate and table from ABC Carpet & Home.

Manufactured in the United States of America
10   9   8   7   6   5   4   3   2   1

To family and friends who have given me love and encouragement.

CONTENTS

ACKNOWLEDGMENTS

I would like to thank several people who helped me with this project. First of all, I want to say thank you to my agent, Linda Hayes, who believed in me enough to stick with this book until it saw the light of day. Thank you also to Tony Cenicola for the superb photography. Thanks to my editor, Justin Schwartz, who kept me on the straight and narrow. I owe a debt of gratitude to Jana Reavis, who was there from the beginning. A thank you also to Ruth Caruana for her encouragement. Lastly, I want to thank Bob Marean for his theories of Zen and the art of computer maintenance.

FOREWORD

Flavored oils, vinegars, and sherries can transform a dish from the ordinary to the extraordinary. They can serve as the foundation of a classic recipe or the final fillip of flavor splashed on at the last moment.

Imagine: what would Szechwan chicken taste like without a dash of chili oil? Or what better way to counter the boring blandness of a poached chicken breast than with a spritz of tarragon vinegar? Plain roast beef? Garlicky cayenne-sherry sauce adds a burst of hot spiciness.

Popular restaurants and grocery stores are stocking an increasingly abundant variety of these magical elixirs. What many people don't know, however, is that making flavored oils, vinegars, and sherries is easy, fun, and satisfying. No special equipment or ingredients are required, and it requires very little time. You can choose from the freshest of ingredients, tailored to your own taste. And best of all, it's a back-to-basics, hands-on approach to making an everyday dish new, fresh, and exciting.

INTRODUCTION

An Oil, Vinegar, and Sherry Primer

OILS

Oils, that is liquid fats, serve a variety of culinary functions. They serve as catalysts in the cooking process, transferring heat from the flame to the food, making it possible to brown food without drying it out. They also serve as flavoring agents and lubricants, such as in a simple, classic vinaigrette. Fats are also indispensable in baking because they tame the gluten present in varying amounts in most flour, thus making pastries flaky and breads light. Knowing how something works lets you make intelligent decisions about when and how to use it.

There are two basic methods for obtaining fats and oils from their animal and vegetable sources: rendering and extraction.

Rendering is simply a matter of heating animal tissue until the fat liquefies and separates from the muscle tissue and its liquids. Extraction, on the other hand, can involve any of three methods: cold pressing, heat extraction, and chemical extraction.

Cold pressing is by far the most desirable means of extracting oils from their vegetable sources. In this process the vegetable source (such as seeds or nuts) is subjected to pressure to break down the cell walls and allow the oil to escape. The most desirable means of accomplishing this is by using a hydraulic press without the addition of any heat. This is what is meant by the term "cold-pressed." Oil obtained by this method is referred to as "extra virgin," meaning that no heat or chemical solvent was used in its extraction. Oil, like wine, is a living thing and the less that is done to it the better.

Pressing with the addition of heat, up to 200°F, can substantially increase the yield of the oil from a vegetable source, which is why this method is popular among oil manufacturers. Although oil obtained in this way should not be considered adulterated, and can, in fact, be suitable for some culinary purposes, it cannot be labeled extra virgin and is certainly less desirable than its cold-pressed cousin.

The third, and least desirable, method of extracting oil is with the addition of hydrocarbon solvents. The word "solvent" is not usually one associated with fine food.

Although the process, chemically speaking, is not as bizarre as it might at first seem, and does, in fact account for much of the edible oil produced today, it does not yield the kind of oil that a good cook would want to use with any regularity.

Hydrocarbon solvents are used because they can dissolve fat. Because they are also volatile they can be removed by heat after they have served their purpose. Oil produced in this manner has the distinction of not only having been heated, probably more than once, but also of containing minute amounts of the solvent that was used in the extraction process. From a health standpoint, the traces of solvent are probably insignificant, but certainly this oil could never be considered "unadulterated."

In the oil trade, oils which are cold-pressed, or at most extracted with a only a minimal amount of heat, are referred to as unrefined. Oils which are extracted with the use of chemical solvents are called refined. Besides the obvious, there are other qualities that separate unrefined oils from their refined cousins.

Unrefined oils have a tendency to cloud at lower temperatures. Place a jar of olive oil in the refrigerator and in a short time and the oil becomes viscous and opaque. At room temperature, unrefined oils have a darker, richer color. They also have more aroma and flavor reminiscent of their source. Minimally processed peanut oil, for example, actually smells like freshly roasted peanuts. Olive oil has a distinct perfume that harkens back to the particular species of olive from which it was extracted. Furthermore, unrefined oils retain more of their natural nutrients, such as vitamin E. Because unrefined oils have a lower flash point (the temperature at which they burst into flame) than refined oils, they are not as well suited to high-temperature cooking, but rather are best pressed into service as a flavor enhancer to finished or raw foods.

Only a small number of plant species actually yield usable oil in any significant quantity, and an even smaller number yield edible oil. Here is a list of the most commonly used culinary oils.

Almond
Avocado
Canola (Rapeseed)
Coconut
Corn
Cottonseed
Grapeseed
Hazelnut
Olive
Peanut
Rice Bran
Safflower
Sesame
Soybean
Sunflower
Walnut

Properties of Commonly Used Culinary Oils

Almond oil.
Oil extracted from the nut of the almond tree has a distinct aroma and flavor of toasted

almonds. All nuts that are used for oil production must first be toasted to intensify their natural flavors. Almond oil is used extensively in baking where an almond flavor is desired.

Avocado oil.

This oil is extracted from the fruit of the avocado tree. As unrefined oils go, avocado oil is quite bland. It is a healthy choice but its characteristics and cost limit its usefulness.

Canola (rapeseed) oil.

Canola oil is currently enjoying a surge in popularity because of its relatively high percentage of unsaturated fat. Canola oil is virtually tasteless and odorless. Some people might be confused by the fact that canola oil, which comes from the rapeseed plant, is considered edible. Rapeseed oil was historically considered toxic because of its high concentration of erucic acid. Canadian plant breeders, however, developed low erucic acid rapeseed and it is from this strain that the oil is extracted.

Coconut oil.

This oil has the distinction of being one of the highest in saturated fat. Because it is cheap it is used extensively in the commercial food industry, although many food producers are getting away from it because of the intense negative publicity it has received of late. A jar of coconut oil on the shelf is virtually indistinguishable in appearance from a jar of rendered lard. It is, in fact, more highly saturated than lard.

Corn oil.

If you can find unrefined corn oil in health food store or gourmet shop, buy it. It is redolent of freshly roasted corn on the cob. The preponderance of corn oil sold, however, is refined and therefore lacks a distinct corn aroma and flavor. It does retain the natural golden hue of ripe corn. It is a good all-purpose oil for cooking purposes.

Cottonseed oil.

Because it is plentiful, and therefore inexpensive, cottonseed oil was long a darling of the food-processing industry. It is often found in generic "vegetable oil" blends. Except for its low cost, however, it has little to recommend it, lacking character as well as any nutritional value.

Grapeseed oil.

This oil is becoming increasingly more common in gourmet food shops. It has been popular in Europe for a long time. If you've ever smelled the Italian brandy grappa, which is made from grape seeds, stems, and wine pressings, then you have a fair idea of what this oil smells like. It is an interesting specialty oil.

Hazelnut oil.

This oil has a distinct aroma and flavor of roasted hazelnuts. Like all nut oils, it tends to have a shorter shelf life than many other oils, but its color, flavor, and scent make it an interesting boutique oil.

Olive oil.

Of all vegetable oils, olive oil certainly has to rank as number one in popularity and usefulness. Olive oils come in a rainbow of hues, from the lightest straw color to earthy green. They come in flavor intensities ranging from the most modest hint of olive to bold, assertive, and vibrant.

Over the years, especially since the gourmet food explosion of the seventies and eighties, olive oils of various origin and variety have battled for top billing as the darling of the in-the-know food set. French oil reigns supreme one year, Italian another, Spanish yet another, and, lately, California olive oils have taken center stage.

According to standards established in Europe, olive oils are classified according to the amount of acidity they contain. The lower the acid level, the finer the oil. In ascending order of acidity, olive oils are classified as extra virgin, super fine virgin, fine virgin, virgin and, simply, olive oil.

Palm oil.

Like coconut oil, this is highly saturated. Because it is inexpensive it is widely used in commercial food products, although because of consumer resistance its use is waning.

Peanut oil.

The best peanut oil has a redolent smell of freshly roasted peanuts. Peanut oil is almost always found in its refined state and is the oil of choice for oriental cooking.

Pumpkinseed oil.

Pumpkinseed oil is usually available only in health food stores and gourmet food shops. It is not suitable for cooking although its rich flavor readily lends it use in salads and wherever it need not be heated.

Rice bran oil.

Rice bran oil has recently become more available in this country. It has always been popular in Japan. It actually has very little to recommend it except that some people find its flavor interesting.

Safflower oil.

Safflower oil is popular in vegetable oil blends and in margarines. It has a relatively high percentage of poly- and monounsaturates. It has virtually no color or taste which makes it suitable in recipes where fat is a necessary ingredient but where its flavor would be a detraction.

Sesame oil.

Derived from sesame seeds, sesame oil has always been popular in oriental cuisines. Toasted sesame oil has a dark color and a deep, rich flavor that predominates in any dish in which it used.

Soybean oil.

Soybean oil is used extensively in commercial food preparation because of its availability and cost. It has virtually no color or flavor. There are many better choices for cooking purposes.

Sunflower oil.

Sunflower oil is readily available, inexpensive, and has a relatively high percentage of polyunsaturates. It is an excellent choice for an all-purpose cooking oil.

Walnut oil.

This oil is very fragrant and has recently become a "boutique" oil, used in gourmet recipes and upscale restaurants. Walnut oil is not as stable as most vegetable oils and is best stored under refrigeration.

VINEGARS

Although definitely not as glamorous, vinegar owes its existence to wine. *Vinaigre*, in French, means "sour wine." Vinegar is the result of the fermentation of alcohol by a certain species of bacteria. When acetobacter bacteria interact with alcohol, they produce enzymes that oxidize the alcohol and the result is vinegar. Simply defined, vinegar is a dilute solution of acetic acid. The most common dilutions are in the 4 to 8 percent range.

Vinegar, in one guise or another, is as common in most cultures as salt and pepper. Its acidic quality makes it useful as a tenderizer, a preserver, and as a condiment. Vinegar has been around for more than five thousand years, and has been produced commercially for about the last five hundred years.

Acids have the ability to break down the proteins in meat. Although this tenderizing action occurs mostly at the surface, by poking holes in the meat, and thus allowing the marinade to seep into the tissue, the tenderizing action can take place beneath the surface as well.

Vinegar is an excellent preservative. Combined with salt to form a brine, its low pH creates an inhospitable environment for most of the microbes that spoil food.

Vinegar's use as a condiment predates Greek and Roman times. At some point before the middle ages, people began flavoring their vinegars with various herbs, spices, fruits, and berries.

There are many different kinds of vinegars available commercially. Here is a list of the most readily available ones.

Balsamic vinegar.
Authentic balsamic vinegar comes only from Modena, Italy. It is made from the cooked juice of the Trebbiano grape. Its characteristic dark color comes from the aging it undergoes in wooden casks over a period of years. Although once rare and expensive, balsamic vinegar has become readily available lately. It has a pungent, sweet taste.

Cane vinegar.
Popular in the Philippines, cane vinegar is relatively low in acid and is made from sugar cane.

Champagne vinegar.
An excellent choice for making flavored vinegars because it has a very mild flavor. It is made from the same grapes used to make champagne.

Cider vinegar.
Made from apple cider, and popular in pickling recipes because of its fruity taste.

Malt vinegar.
In Great Britain, vinegar means malt vinegar. Authentic malt vinegar is made from beer or ale. Its malty flavor makes it a good choice for sauces and it is the condiment of choice for traditional fish and chips.

Red wine vinegar.

Made from a variety of red wines, depending on its origin. It has a full-bodied flavor which marries well with olive oil in classic Italian-style vinaigrette, and is also a good choice for marinades.

Rice vinegar.

Very popular in oriental cuisine, especially Japanese cuisine. It is made from rice and comes in both flavored and unflavored varieties. The unflavored version is used as a condiment in sushi bars. The flavored variety tends to be rather sweet and, depending on the brand, can make a good choice for sprinkling on steamed rice or for use in a salad dressing.

Sherry vinegar.

Made from sherry wine. Originally from Spain, some is now produced in this country. Like sherry, this vinegar is aged in wooden casks and has a distinctive sherrylike flavor.

White vinegar.

The vodka of the vinegar world. It is distilled from grain alcohol, has no color and no distinctive flavor other than that of acetic acid. It is the most popular vinegar in commercial pickle products.

White wine vinegar.

Made from a variety of white wines depending on its origin. It is an excellent choice for making herb-flavored vinegars.

SHERRY

Like champagne, real sherry, by definition, comes only from a certain part of the world, namely the Jerez (pronounced *haireth*) region of Spain. Like champagne, sherry-style wines are produced around the world and some of the pretenders are actually better than some examples of the real thing.

Sherry is a fortified wine. The fermenting, aging, and blending process is part of what makes sherry unique and what makes for the several different varieties of sherries.

The Jerez district of Spain lies in the southwest corner of the country, near the Portuguese border. Three keys to making sherry are the soil, the climate, and the grape variety. Unlike much of Spain, the soil is chalky-white and the climate is hot and dry. The third ingredient that goes into making sherry is the grape—the Palomino. All varieties of sherry are made from this single grape.

Because the climate is so warm, the Palomino grape ripens on the vine to a very high sugar content. As is common in Mediterranean countries, after the grapes are picked they are spread out in the sun to dry slightly, further concentrating the sugar content.

After the grapes are crushed they ferment rapidly. The high sugar content translates into a high alcohol content, approaching 15 or 16 percent. The wine is laid to rest in casks for a period of several months. Even though all the wine is a product of the same grapes, wine in different casks begins to take on different characteristics. Unlike most still wines that are poured into barrels to the very top to seal out all air, sherry wine barrels are filled so as to leave a space for air above the wine. This results in some of the barrels developing a *flor*, which is a mask or veil that forms on the surface of the wine. The flor is a natural yeast. This yeast, and the fact that sherries are allowed to come in contact with air while they are in the barrel, give them their unique characteristics. Other wines of lower alcohol content would probably spoil before they had a chance to age if they were allowed to oxygenate in this manner.

Because of the way sherries are blended, there is no such thing as a vintage sherry. The blending process is known as the *solera* method. Wine casks are stacked one upon the other in a pyramid fashion. The casks at the top hold the youngest wine. Those at the very bottom, the oldest. The bottom casks, as a matter of fact, can, and usually do, contain some very old sherry. How old depends on how high the particular *solera* is and when it was begun. Since the more venerable sherry producers have been around for centuries, the age of the wine in some of these barrels can be considerable.

The blending process begins when some wine is drawn off from the bottom-most barrels and bottled. It is replaced with wine from the barrels directly above, which in turn is replaced by wine from the barrels above those, and so on. As the younger wine is introduced into the barrels below it quickly begins taking on the characteristics of its more mature cousin.

Sherries are divided into categories according to their residual sugar content, color, and flavor. The good news about all sherries is that it is quite easy to find an excellent sherry at a very reasonable price. The driest and palest are called *finos*. Of the finos, the *manzanillas* are the driest and most delicately flavored.

In the middle range of dryness and color are the *amontillados*, made famous in the Edgar Allen Poe short story that owes its title to their name. Amontillados tend have a somewhat nutty flavor and are darker, sweeter, and softer than the finos.

At the other end of the spectrum are the *olorosos*. These sherries are full-flavored, can be quite dark in color, and because they are aged longer, tend to be more expensive. Olorosos can further be divided into subcategories. *Dry oloroso* is not very common since most oloroso is sweetened and made into cream sherry. It has a magnificent depth of flavor and bouquet. *Sweet oloroso* is a complex sherry whose sweetness is an adjunct to its flavor and not a mask to cover up any deficiencies. The sweetness is achieved by adding concentrated grape juice to the wine. This is another technique popular among wine makers in Mediterranean countries to give their wine fuller body and flavor.

Palo cortados fall somewhere in between amontillados and olorosos. They have characteristics of both but definitely tend to be a little more like olorosos. They are quite rare because most of the sherries would tend to fall into one of the other three main categories.

Cream sherries tend to be the sweetest. More often than not, the sweetness merely serves as a cover-up for the wine's character flaws. Pale cream sherry is more a marketing ploy than a unique category of sherry. It is actually sweetened fino sherry.

Because sherries are fortified with additional alcohol (except for the delicate finos), they are very hardy. An opened bottle can usually be kept at room temperature, stoppered, of course, for several months without any serious deleterious effects. Refrigeration would actually prevent you from tasting some of the more complex and subtle flavors in some of the better sherries.

As a vehicle for flavoring, you don't need to search out the best and most expensive sherries. Certainly anything that is drinkable will do. Fortunately, since sherries are quite reasonably priced, a good quality sherry needn't be a luxury when preparing to make a flavored variety.

PART ONE

Making Flavored Oils, Vinegars, and Sherries

Flavored oils, vinegars, and sherries have been around for centuries. Ethnic cuisines have used them extensively for flavoring and, to a lesser extent, as preservatives.

The equipment needed to produce a high-quality product is basic to any kitchen. The techniques required are no more difficult than boiling an egg. Anyone who is willing to invest a little time is assured of producing a product at least as good as, if not better than, anything commercially available.

Utensils

Only basic kitchen equipment is required. Saucepans for heating liquids are the most obvious. Depending on the amount of flavored infusions you anticipate making, a two- or three-quart pan should suffice. Measuring spoons and cups are a necessity.

Kitchen shears and a sharp chopping knife for preparing herbs are also requisite. This is one area you shouldn't skimp on. A quality knife and shears will last a lifetime with proper care. A food processor can come in handy, as can a coffee grinder, for chopping herbs and spices, but you can do just as well without them if necessary.

Containers

Certainly you can get by with virtually any recycled jar or bottle that you can seal tightly. For fancier presentations, however, some quality bottles that come with cork stoppers or Mason-jar-style wire and rubber washer closures make excellent choices. Sizes are purely an individual matter, depending on the amount of infusions you intend to make. Bottles can be clear or any color you wish, except that clear glass usually shows off your finished product in its best light.

Techniques

No special techniques are required. One thing that cannot be overstressed, however, is cleanliness. In order to assure a high-quality product, great care and attention should be paid to keeping all equipment and containers that will in any way come into contact with food scrupulously clean.

Sterilizing containers in a hot water bath is a good idea but probably is not absolutely necessary as long as everything is washed in detergent and rinsed well in hot water. If in doubt, always err on the side of caution. Nothing contributes more to a spoiled product than a lack of cleanliness.

All fresh herbs that are used should be thoroughly rinsed in cold, running water and dried completely in layers of paper towels. Only the highest quality dried herbs and spices should be used.

The Safety Issue

Anytime we combine different ingredients and pack them away for storage for use at a later time, there is always the possibility that some form of contamination can lead to food spoilage. Fortunately, vinegar and alcohol

are excellent preservatives and there is little chance that any infusions made from these two liquids will spoil if given the most basic care in preparation and storage.

A question arises, however, about oil infusions. First of all, let me say that oil infusions have been around a very long time; they have, as we learned earlier, been a part of the cuisines of many cultures in many different guises. But because oils don't have the same preservative qualities as vinegar and alcohol, storing your infusions in a cool, even cold place can't hurt.

Ingredients

Ingredients for infusions fall into two categories: the base liquid (oil, vinegar, or sherry) and the added ingredients (herbs, spices, and other flavoring ingredients).

Oils.
Unless a recipe specifies a specific oil, feel free to choose from any top-quality vegetable oil, but generally your safest choices are peanut, corn, and olive oils. Corn oil has the mildest taste but both peanut and olive can add resonance to a flavored oil, depending on the other ingredients.

Widely available brands of peanut oil tend to be rather bland. You might do well to search out oriental groceries, health food stores, and gourmet specialty shops to find a peanut oil that has a "peanuttier" flavor.

In recipes that call for sesame oil, this specifically refers to the oriental-style toasted sesame oil. If you are willing to experiment try a few different brands. Generally speaking, you will find prices most reasonable in oriental groceries.

Vinegars.
Here again, unless a recipe specifies (and most do), feel free to use whatever vinegar you think would taste good with a particular combination of ingredients. You usually can't go wrong with any name-brand distilled white or cider vinegar. There are also several name-brand red and white wine and champagne vinegars available, but there are also lesser known brands, some imported, that are excellent. Again, experiment to find what you like best.

As far as rice wine vinegar is concerned, one brand stands out for flavor and quality: *Marukan*. Generally the unseasoned variety is the best choice, but this brand also has a seasoned variety that you should try. Some may not like the particular combination of sweetness and spice but for some recipes I find it the perfect go-along.

Sherries.
As was noted earlier, you don't need to spend a fortune to obtain a high-quality sherry. Any imported or domestic sherry that you find pleasurably drinkable is certainly good enough to use in your infusions. Unless a recipe specifies, and again, most do, try to stick with a dry cocktail-type sherry.

Aromatics.
Aromatics include herbs, spices, citrus peel, garlic, ginger, shallots, and lemon grass. Dried herbs and spices should be pungent

with natural flavor and aroma. Buy from sources you trust (or grow your own when possible).

Citrus should be washed in a mild solution of dish detergent and water and rinsed well under warm running water. Most citrus that finds its way to your grocer's shelves has been sprayed with fungicides, insecticides, or worse. Washing the fruit removes at least some of these chemicals.

Garlic and shallots should be very fresh. Garlic should be peeled and scored before adding to a recipe. If you want to be extra safe, you can soak garlic and shallots in some distilled white vinegar before adding it to an oil infusion. (Just be sure to dry it thoroughly before adding it to the oil.) Shallots should be peeled, as should ginger. Lemon grass should be very fresh and smell pungently lemony when you bruise it slightly.

CHAPTER ONE

Flavored Oils

Flavored oils provide a fantastic way to add flavor and excitement to foods without adding a significant amount of fat or calories. Granted, all oils are fat and so all contain calories. But because they are flavored, a little goes a long way. By using different base oils and different combinations of herbs and spices, we can create countless exciting taste and flavor variations, suitable for inclusion in myriad recipes.

Because of the safety considerations discussed in the previous chapter, it's important to follow the recipes precisely and to exercise extra care and caution. If you wish, you can refrigerate the finished products as an added precaution. If you do so, remember that certain oils, like olive and peanut, become cloudy and quite viscous at refrigerator temperatures. Although this in no way detracts from the quality or flavor of the product, it certainly does detract from its appearance and so it's best to let them come to room temperature before serving.

As you become more experienced in making your own infusions, you might want to experiment with different combinations of base oils and ingredients. Your imagination is your only limit.

Allspice and Bay Oil

This oil has a wonderful perfume that marries well with poultry or veal. Allspice is a favorite in central European countries in both meat dishes and desserts. If you have access to a laurel tree, the fresh leaves are superior to anything you'll find in a can or jar, but the dried variety will do.

2 cups corn or peanut oil
¼ cup whole allspice berries
8 to 10 bay leaves
1 teaspoon whole black peppercorns

Heat the oil in a 2-quart saucepan to a temperature of 225° to 250°F. Add the remaining ingredients and turn off the heat. Allow the mixture to come to room temperature and then bottle in clean jars or bottles. If dividing it among several containers, make sure some of the solids are added to each one. Store at cool room temperature. When using the oil,

it's probably wise to keep the solids, especially the bay leaves, in the bottle. Bay leaves have been known to be very rough on the digestive system.

Anise Oil

Anise is a member of the parsley family and has been a favorite of Mediterranean and Asian cuisines for centuries. The seed has a distinctly sweet licorice flavor.

2 cups corn oil
½ cup anise seed

In a 2-quart saucepan, heat the oil to a temperature of 225° to 250°F. Add the anise seed and keep the oil over a very low flame for about 5 minutes. Do not allow the temperature to rise above 250°F. Remove from the heat and allow the oil to come to room temperature. Strain the oil through cheesecloth or a coffee filter into clean jars or bottles. Store in a cool place.
Note: For a wonderfully different flavor, substitute star anise for the regular anise seed.

Chili Pepper Oil

Chili pepper oils fall into two basic categories: Mediterranean and Asian. This recipe is for a decidedly oriental-style oil that goes well with stir-fries.

2 cups peanut oil
¼ cup crushed dried red peppers (from cayenne or Thai bird peppers)
¼ cup fennel seed
1 tablespoon Szechwan peppercorns

Heat the oil in a 2-quart saucepan to 225° to 250°F. Add the remaining ingredients and remove the pan from the heat. Allow the oil to come to room temperature. Scoop out the solids and divide them and the oil into clean jars or bottles and store at a cool temperature.

Chili Oil with Garlic

This is another oil that goes well with oriental foods, especially Thai or Korean cuisines.

2 cups peanut oil
¼ cup crushed dried red peppers
4 cloves garlic, peeled and scored
1 tablespoon anise seed
1 tablespoon whole black peppercorns

Heat the oil in a 2-quart saucepan to 225° to 250°F. Add the remaining ingredients and remove from the heat. Allow the oil to come to room temperature. Remove the garlic cloves. Scoop out the solids and divide them and the oil among clean bottles or jars. Store at a cool temperature.

Clove Oil

This aromatic oil goes well with beef stew and chicken or meat stocks and is the perfect addition to sautéed or caramelized onions. It also adds a new dimension to fruit salads.

2 cups corn oil
½ cup whole cloves

Heat the oil in a 2-quart saucepan to 225° to 250°F. Add the cloves and allow the oil to bubble gently over a low flame for 10 minutes. Do not allow the temperature to rise above 250°F. Remove from the heat and let the oil come to room temperature. Scoop out the solids and divide them and the oil among clean jars or bottles. Store in a cool place.

Curry Oil

This oil is an exciting, complex panoply of flavors. One of the more interesting ingredients is cardamom seed, which, though expensive, has a wonderful, pungent aroma and a spicy-sweet flavor. This oil makes a splendid addition to East Indian dishes and curries of all kinds.

4 cups peanut or corn oil
¼ cup cardamom seed, crushed slightly in a mortar and pestle or coarsely ground in a coffee grinder
¼ cup crushed dried red peppers
1 teaspoon yellow mustard seed
1 tablespoon cumin seed
1 tablespoon whole black peppercorns
One 2- to 3-inch stick cinnamon, broken into small pieces
1 tablespoon whole cloves
2 tablespoons coarsely chopped fresh ginger
1 tablespoon fennel seed
1 tablespoon fenugreek
1 tablespoon celery seed

Heat the oil in a 3-quart saucepan to 225° to 250°F. Add the remaining ingredients and remove from the heat. Allow the oil to come to room temperature. Strain the mixture through several layers of cheesecloth and

divide among clean jars or bottles. Store at a cool temperature.

Dill Oil

Dill seed has a more pungent flavor than the leaves of the plant. Heating brings out its flavor even more. Try this oil with meat, poultry, and fish dishes.

2 cups corn oil
¾ cup dill seed

Heat the oil in a 2-quart saucepan to 225° to 250°F. Add the dill seed and keep over a low flame for 5 minutes. Strain the mixture through several layers of cheesecloth and divide among clean jars or bottles. Store in a cool place.

Fennel Oil

Greenish-brown fennel seeds have a delicate, slightly sweet licorice flavor that marries well with shellfish, seafood, meats, and salads of mixed greens. Substitute some fennel oil for plain oil in a simple vinaigrette for a subtly unique flavor enhancement.

2 cups extra virgin olive oil
½ cup fennel seed
1 tablespoon whole black peppercorns

Heat the oil in a 2-quart saucepan to 225° to 250°F. Coarsely chop the fennel seed with a mortar and pestle or in a food processor. Add them and the peppercorns to the oil. Remove from the heat and let cool to room temperature. Strain the oil through several layers of cheesecloth and divide among clean bottles or jars. Store in a cool place.

Oil with Fines Herbes

The classic fines herbes combination is chervil, parsley, chives, and tarragon, often supplemented with marjoram, savory, and sometimes watercress and burnet. This oil is delicately flavored and can be used in many recipes calling for fines herbes. It should be added close to the end of cooking time because the flavors will disappear quickly when heated.

2 cups extra virgin olive oil
¼ cup fresh tarragon
¼ cup fresh chervil
1 cup fresh parsley
1 cup fresh chives
¼ cup fresh marjoram

Wash the herbs and dry them thoroughly. Place the herbs in a wide mouth jar and pour the oil over them. Cover and allow to infuse for 2 weeks in a cool place. Remove the herbs and divide the oil among clean jars or bottles.

Ginger Spice Oil

This is a spicy, fiery oil that goes well with Asian or Indian dishes. A little goes a long way.

2 cups peanut oil
¼ cup chopped fresh ginger
Two 2- to 3-inch cinnamon sticks, broken into small pieces

¼ cup crushed dried cayenne peppers
¼ cup coriander seed, coarsely crushed
¼ cup cumin seed, coarsely crushed

Heat the oil in a 2-quart saucepan to 225° to 250°F. Add the remaining ingredients and keep the oil over a low flame for 5 to 10 minutes. Do not allow the oil to rise above 250°F. Remove from heat and allow the oil to come to room temperature. Strain the mixture through several layers of cheesecloth and divide among clean bottles or jars.

Green Herb Oil

You can experiment with the combination of herbs in this oil. This recipe is just a starting point. Use your imagination!

2 cups extra virgin olive oil
4 sprigs fresh thyme
4 sprigs fresh tarragon
4 sprigs fresh rosemary
4 fresh sage leaves
4 sprigs fresh marjoram
5 to 6 bay leaves
1 tablespoon whole black peppercorns

Wash the herbs and dry thoroughly. Place the herbs in a wide-mouth jar and pour the oil over them. Close and allow to infuse for 2 weeks in a cool, dark place. Remove the herbs and divide the oil among clean bottles or jars. A fresh sprig of any of the ingredient herbs and a bay leaf in each bottle will give great eye appeal. Store in a cool place.

Lemon Thyme Oil

Lemon thyme is a delightful herb that combines the slightly minty aroma of thyme with an accent of lemon. It is also a very pretty herb. The usual gray-green thyme leaves have a pretty yellow border. If you can't find any lemon thyme, feel free to use regular thyme. With the addition of the lemon peel, you won't notice any difference in flavor. A sprig of lemon thyme in the finished product, however, will add definite eye appeal.

2 cups extra virgin olive oil
1 cup fresh lemon thyme (or thyme) leaves and
  stems
1 large lemon

Wash the thyme and dry thoroughly. Wash the lemon in warm water and a mild dish detergent. Rinse completely and dry thoroughly. Using a vegetable peeler remove all the peel from the lemon. Put the thyme and lemon peel in a wide-mouth jar and pour the oil over them. Close and allow to infuse in a cool, dark place for 2 weeks. Remove the thyme and lemon peel and divide among clean bottles or jars.

Pizza Oil

This is a great oil to drizzle on pizza just before you pop it in the oven. Try it on veggies and fish or poultry too.

2 cups extra virgin olive oil
4 sprigs fresh oregano
4 sprigs fresh basil
4 sprigs fresh thyme

2 tablespoons whole black peppercorns
2 tablespoons crushed dried red pepper

Wash the herbs and dry thoroughly. Place the herbs, peppercorns, and red pepper in a wide-mouth jar. Pour the oil over them and cover. Allow to infuse for 2 weeks. Remove the herbs and strain the oil through several layers of cheesecloth to remove the peppercorns and red pepper and divide among clean bottles or jars.

Provençal Oil

Provençal refers to dishes prepared in the tradition of Provence in France. Tomatoes, garlic, onions, olives and olive oil, mushrooms, anchovies, and eggplant all play a prominent role in the cuisine of this region. This oil infusion marries well with all of these foodstuffs.

2 cups extra virgin olive oil
4 sprigs fresh thyme
4 sprigs fresh marjoram
4 sprigs fresh summer savory
4 sprigs fresh basil
1 tablespoon whole black peppercorns
6 cloves garlic, peeled and crushed

Wash the herbs and dry thoroughly. Place the herbs, peppercorns, and garlic in a wide-mouth jar and pour the oil over them. Cover and allow to infuse for 2 weeks in a cool dark place. Remove the herbs and strain the oil through several layers of cheesecloth to remove the peppercorns and garlic. Divide among clean bottles or jars, cover and store in a cool place.

Red Pepper Olive Oil

Called *pepperolio* in Italy, this infusion is an excellent substitute for plain olive oil wherever a little bite is called for. The quality of the olive oil you use will determine how good the end result is, but you needn't spend extravagant sums of money for the finest extra virgin oil because the red pepper has a very assertive flavor. Do use a good quality oil, however.

2 cups good quality olive oil
1 cup crushed dried red peppers
¼ cup whole black peppercorns

Heat the oil to 225° to 250°F. Add the red and black pepper and keep the mixture over a low flame for 5 minutes. Do not allow the temperature to rise. Remove from heat and allow the oil to cool to room temperature. Bottle the oil and scoop some of the "goop" into each bottle. The oil will continue to get better with age. Store in a cool place.

Sesame Oil with Szechwan Peppercorns

Toasted sesame oil is a hallmark of oriental cuisine. By adding the flavor of Szechwan peppercorns we can give the oil a piquant bite.

2 cups toasted sesame oil
1 cup crushed Szechwan peppercorns
¼ cup anise seed

Heat the oil to 225° to 250°F. Add the remaining ingredients and remove from the heat. Allow the oil to come to room temperature, strain it through several layers of cheesecloth, and bottle. Store in a cool place.

Thyme Oil

This oil is perfect for fish or poultry. Added to a simple vinaigrette it is also just the right touch for steamed asparagus or broccoli.

2 cups good quality olive oil
8 to 10 sprigs fresh thyme

Wash the thyme and dry it thoroughly. Place the thyme in a jar. Pour the oil into the jar and cover. Allow the oil to infuse for about 2 weeks in a cool place before using it.

CHAPTER TWO

Flavored Vinegars

Flavored vinegars have been around for centuries. They are great for perking up dishes that might otherwise fall into the ho-hum category. And they can do it by adding absolutely no fat and virtually no calories.

Flavor combinations are almost endless. By varying the base vinegar (such as wine, rice, cider, etc.) and the flavoring ingredients, just the right flavor match for just about any food is almost a certainty. Flavoring ingredients can be herbs, spices, or fruits, or any combination of the three.

Making your own flavored vinegars makes good economic sense. Cruise the gourmet aisle in your local grocery sometime and get a load of what they're charging these days for tossing a couple raspberries into some mediocre wine vinegar. Raspberries tend to be a little expensive, granted, but not nearly as expensive as a pint of raspberry wine vinegar would have you believe.

One nice thing about making flavored vinegars is that you don't need to concern yourself with any major health considerations. Vinegar is a natural preservative be-

cause of its low pH, and ordinary common sense rules of cleanliness in food preparation should suffice to turn out a superior product.

Although techniques for making vinegar infusions vary, the simplest methods are usually the best. The recipes here should be viewed as starting points. Once you've tried a few, use your imagination and concoct some of your own. And try these vinegars on several different types of food to see what goes best with what. Some are best splashed on fresh fruit or vegetables. Some might be better wedded to a soup or stew. Be imaginative and creative and you're sure to surprise yourself, as well as your dinner company, with some truly magical flavor combinations.

Flavored vinegars make marvelous gifts. They are easy to make. They are inexpensive. And they show thoughtfulness and caring because they are made by hand.

Although most flavored vinegars might seemingly last forever, they are best used within a year. They should also be stored in a cool, dark place, like a pantry. Heat and light tend to destroy the delicate flavors after a time.

Here then are some flavorful combinations to get you started.

Blackberry Vinegar

The time to make this vinegar is when blackberries are at their peak of ripeness.

4 cups blackberries, slightly bruised
¼ cup bruised mint leaves
4 cups red or white wine vinegar

Wash the fruit and mint leaves and dry thoroughly. Place the berries and leaves in a 2-quart or larger jar. Pour the vinegar over the fruit and leaves and cover. Place the jar in a cool, dark place for 2 weeks. Strain the vinegar through several layers of cheesecloth into clean, sterile bottles or jars and cover. Store in a cool, dark place.

Cinque Herbes Vinegar

This five-herb-flavored vinegar is excellent when splashed on freshly steamed vegetables for that extra little fillip of flavor.

½ cup fresh basil leaves
½ cup fresh oregano leaves
½ cup fresh thyme sprigs
½ cup fresh marjoram leaves
6 to 8 bay leaves
4 cups white wine vinegar

Wash the fresh herbs and dry thoroughly. Place the herbs and bay leaves in a 2-quart or larger sealable jar. Pour the vinegar over the herbs and cover. Store in a cool, dark place for 2 weeks. Strain the vinegar through

several layers of cheesecloth into clean, sterile jars and cover. You may wish to add a sprig of fresh herb to each bottle before you close them. Store in a cool, dark place.

Dill Vinegar

This is the vinegar to make when the dill in your herb patch is at its peak, before it forms flower heads.

1 large bunch fresh dill, about 2 cups
4 cups champagne vinegar

Wash and dry the dill and place it in a large glass jar. Add the vinegar, cover, and store in a cool, dark place for 2 weeks. Add a fresh sprig of dill to each of several clean bottles. Strain the vinegar through several layers of cheesecloth into the bottles, cover, and store in a cool, dark place.

Fines Herbes Vinegar

Fines herbes is a classic French combination of chervil, chives, parsley, and tarragon. Marjoram and savory can also be added to make this herbal medley even more intriguing.

½ cup fresh chervil
½ cup fresh chives
½ cup fresh parsley
½ cup fresh tarragon
½ cup fresh marjoram
½ cup fresh savory
4 cups white wine vinegar

Wash all the herbs and pat dry. Put them in a 2-quart or larger sealable jar. Pour the vinegar over the herbs and cover. Store in a cool,

dark place for 2 weeks. Strain the vinegar through several layers of cheesecloth into clean, sterile jars and close. Store in a cool, dark place.

Garlic Basil Vinegar

Garlic and basil are a natural, classic combination. This vinegar is excellent in a simple vinaigrette, but try it on fresh or steamed vegetables too.

1 head garlic
2 cups fresh basil leaves
4 cups red wine vinegar

Separate the garlic head into individual cloves. Crush the cloves slightly with the flat side of a knife and peel them. Wash the basil leaves and pat dry. Place the basil and garlic in a 2-quart or larger sealable glass jar. Pour the vinegar over the garlic and basil, cover, and store in cool, dark place for 2 weeks. Strain the vinegar through several layers of cheesecloth into clean, sterile bottles and cover. You can add a whole garlic clove or two to each bottle before closing.

Ginger Garlic Vinegar

Ginger and garlic are classic oriental partners. This combination works well in sweet and sour stir-fries or in any dish where a hint of oriental flavor is called for.

1 head garlic
One 4- to 5-inch piece fresh ginger
4 cups white wine vinegar

Separate the head of garlic into individual cloves, crush them with the flat side of a knife, and peel them. Peel the ginger and coarsely chop. Place the garlic and ginger in a 2-quart or larger glass jar. Pour the vinegar over and cover. Store in a cool, dark place for 2 weeks. Strain the vinegar through several layers of cheesecloth into clean, sterile bottles. Store in a cool, dark place.

Ground Hot Pepper Vinegar

This infusion is great for giving meats, soups, and stews a little extra "kick."

1 cup coarsely ground cayenne peppers
1 teaspoon salt
4 cups white wine vinegar

Place the pepper and salt in a large glass jar. Pour the vinegar over and cover. Store in a cool, dark place for 2 weeks. At this point the vinegar may be strained, or not, if you desire. Pour into several smaller bottles and cover.

Lemon Garlic Vinegar

This combination is especially good with fish and poultry.

2 lemons
1 head garlic
4 cups white wine vinegar

With a vegetable peeler remove all the peel from both lemons. Try not to get too much of the underlying white pith as this will

cause some bitterness in the finished product. Separate the head of garlic into cloves, crush them with the flat side of a knife, and peel them. Place the lemon peel and garlic in a large glass jar and pour the vinegar over. Cover and store in a cool, dark place for 2 weeks. Strain the vinegar through several layers of cheesecloth into clean, sterile bottles. A single clove of garlic in each bottle adds a nice visual touch.

Lemon Mint Vinegar

Try this vinegar with any dish you normally associate with lemony or minty flavors.

2 lemons
2 cups fresh mint leaves
¼ cup sugar
4 cups white wine vinegar

Remove the peel from the lemons with a vegetable peeler, being careful to avoid the pith. Wash and dry the mint leaves. Put the sugar in a large glass jar. Pour in the vinegar, cover and shake to dissolve the sugar. Add the lemon peel and mint leaves. Cover and store in a cool, dark place for 2 weeks. Add a fresh sprig of mint to each of several small bottles and strain the vinegar through several layers of cheesecloth into each. Store in a cool, dark place.

North Carolina–style Cayenne Vinegar

If you've ever tasted North Carolina pulled pork barbecue, then you've tasted this vinegar. Along with slow hickory-smoked pork butt, this is what makes "Carolina 'cue."

2 tablespoons sugar
2 teaspoons salt
2 cups apple cider vinegar
2 cups white vinegar
¼ cup crushed red pepper flakes
1 tablespoon paprika
1 tablespoon freshly ground black pepper

Place the sugar and salt in a large glass jar. Add the vinegars, cover, and shake to dissolve. Add the pepper flakes, paprika, and black pepper. This "sauce" can be used immediately, but it gets better with age, and keeps for a very long time (but it probably won't last a long time once you taste it on barbecued pork).

Provençal Vinegar

The cooking of Provence is famous for its reliance on garlic, tomatoes, and olive oil. This infusion goes well with many dishes that include these hallmark ingredients. Try marinating fresh mushrooms in a simple vinaigrette made from one part Provençal vinegar and three parts extra virgin olive oil.

2 tablespoons dried basil
2 tablespoons dried oregano
2 tablespoons dried thyme
2 tablespoons dried marjoram
2 tablespoons whole black peppercorns
1 head garlic
4 cups red wine vinegar

Place the dried herbs and peppercorns in a large glass jar. Separate the head of garlic

into cloves, crush them with the flat side of a knife, and peel them. Add the garlic to the jar. Pour the vinegar over all, cover, and store in a cool, dark place for 2 weeks. Strain the vinegar through several layers of cheesecloth into several clean bottles. A fresh sprig of any of the herbs used in this recipe could be added to each bottle for eye appeal.

Raspberry Lemon Vinegar

Raspberry vinegar has become quite common on grocers' shelves in the past couple of years. Making your own, however, is cheaper and usually better. This recipe adds a fillip of lemon flavor.

2 lemons
2 cups fresh red or black raspberries
¼ cup sugar
4 cups white wine vinegar

Peel the lemons with a vegetable peeler, being careful to avoid the white pith. Wash the raspberries and drain in a colander. Add the sugar to a large glass jar. Pour the vinegar into the jar, cover, and shake to dissolve the sugar. Add the lemon peel and raspberries. Cover and store in a cool, dark place for 2 weeks. Add 3 or 4 fresh raspberries to each of several clean glass bottles and strain the vinegar through several layers of cheesecloth into each bottle. Cover and store in a cool, dark place.

Rice Wine Vinegar with Garlic

Be sure to use unflavored rice wine vinegar for this recipe.

1 head garlic
4 cups unflavored rice wine vinegar

Separate the head of garlic into cloves, crush them with the flat side of a knife, and peel them. Place the cloves in a large glass jar. Pour the vinegar in the jar, cover, and store in cool, dark place for 2 weeks. Add a fresh clove or two of garlic to each of several clean bottles. Strain the vinegar through several layers of cheesecloth into the bottles. Cover and store in a cool, dark place.

Rice Wine Vinegar with Ginger

Ginger and rice vinegar are a natural combination. Use it in any oriental-style recipe that calls for rice vinegar.

One 4- to 5-inch piece fresh ginger
4 cups rice wine vinegar

Peel the ginger and chop it coarsely in a food processor. Put it in a large glass jar. Pour the vinegar over, cover, and store in a cool, dark place for 2 weeks. Strain the vinegar through several layers of cheesecloth into several clean bottles. Cover and store in a cool, dark place.

Rice Wine Vinegar with Lemon Grass and Kaffir Lime

Lemon grass and kaffir lime leaves are staples of Thai and Vietnamese cuisine. They are available in many Asian groceries in this country. Lemon grass is sold by the stalk. Because it is rather woody and fibrous, only the lower base of the stalk is used. Once only available dried, kaffir limes are now being grown in Florida and California and so the leaves and the fruit are often available fresh in oriental groceries. There really is no substitute for either of these ingredients, so if you can't find them you'll just have to skip this recipe.

4 stalks fresh lemon grass
10 fresh kaffir lime leaves
4 cups rice wine vinegar

Cut off the bottom 6 inches or so of the lemon grass. Discard the tops. Coarsely chop the remaining pieces in a food processor. Coarsely shred the kaffir lime leaves. Put the lime leaves and lemon grass in a large jar and add the rice wine vinegar, cover, and store in a cool place for 2 weeks. Strain the vinegar through several layers of cheesecloth into a clean bottle. You can add a fresh stalk of lemon grass to the bottle for a little visual excitement and slightly more flavor and aroma.

Rice Wine Vinegar with Shallots and Herbs

Shallots marry well with many different herbs. Try this vinegar in any basic vinaigrette recipe for a decidedly different flavor.

1 cup shallots
4 to 5 sprigs fresh thyme
4 to 5 sprigs fresh oregano
1 large bunch fresh chives, about 1 cup
4 cups rice wine vinegar

Separate the shallots, peel, and coarsely chop. Wash the fresh herbs and chives and dry thoroughly. Put the herbs and chives in a large glass jar, pour the vinegar over all, cover, and store in a cool, dark place for 2 weeks. Put a whole fresh shallot and 2 or 3 stalks fresh chives in each of several clean glass bottles. Strain the vinegar through several layers of cheesecloth into the bottles, cover and store in a cool, dark place.

Rose Petal Vinegar

Most people don't associate roses with food, but, in fact, rose petals have a very pleasant and very delicate flavor. Use roses from your own garden or from a source that guarantees that they were organically grown. Roses from your local florist are apt to have been sprayed with pesticides. The reddest roses will, of course, yield deepest hued vinegar.

4 cups red rose petals
4 cups white wine or champagne vinegar

Wash the rose petals and dry. Place them in a large glass jar. Pour the vinegar into the jar, cover, and store in a cool, dark place for 2 weeks. Strain the vinegar into clean glass bottles, cover, and store in a cool, dark place. If you desire, you can add a small rosebud to each jar for visual appeal.

Strawberry Vinegar

The flavor of this vinegar marries well with pork and veal, as well as "cool" veggies such as cucumbers and zucchini.

4 cups red, ripe strawberries
4 cups white wine vinegar

Wash the strawberries and drain in a colander. Bruise them slightly and put them in a large glass jar. Pour the vinegar into the jar, cover, and store in cool, dark place for 2 weeks. Place a single red, ripe strawberry in each of several clean bottles and strain the vinegar into each bottle through several layers of cheesecloth. Cover and store in a cool, dark place.

Tarragon Dill Vinegar

Tarragon has a very distinctive flavor and aroma. By adding a little dill to this recipe we tame the tarragon slightly. Try this vinegar in poultry dishes that classically call for a little tarragon flavor. Try it also with fresh veggies, such as asparagus or green beans.

5 to 6 sprigs fresh tarragon
1 large bunch fresh dill, about 1 cup
4 cups white wine vinegar

Wash the tarragon and dill and pat dry. Place the herbs in a large glass jar. Pour the vinegar over the herbs, cover, and store in a cool, dark place for 2 weeks. Place a fresh sprig of tarragon into each of several clean bottles and strain the vinegar into each bottle. Cover and store in a cool, dark place.

CHAPTER THREE

Flavored Sherries

Bermudian sherried pepper sauce is probably the most famous concoction that uses sherry as the base liquid. Other flavoring ingredients can be just as exciting. Depending on the flavoring ingredients, flavored sherries are useful in many main dishes as well as desserts.

When making a flavored sherry, it's important to use a good quality sherry wine. A good rule of thumb is if you wouldn't drink it, then don't use it. Because sherries are fortified with added alcohol, their keeping properties are quite good. But you have to remember, sherries are wines, and as such are living and breathing and therefore will eventually spoil. It's even more important to store them in a cool, dark place, and to use them within about three months after you make them.

As with flavored oils and vinegars, let these recipes be jumping-off points for your imagination.

Allspice-flavored Sherry

Allspice berries are good for flavoring beef, pork, and veal dishes, as well as many different desserts, such as pies, puddings, cakes, and cookies. This sherry should come in handy in many different ways. Allspice berries get their name from the fact that they combine the flavors of cinnamon, nutmeg, and cloves. Most of the berries come from Jamaica, although Central and South America also grow and export a significant amount.

1 bottle slightly sweet sherry
½ cup whole allspice berries

Pour off about 1 cup of sherry and reserve. Add the allspice berries to the remaining sherry and pour back as much of the reserved sherry as will fit in the bottle. Store in a cool, dark place for 2 weeks. The sherry can be strained to remove the berries, or they can be left in the bottle, which will add slightly to the flavor intensity.

Bird Pepper Sherry

If you've never experienced Thai bird peppers, you are definitely in for a treat. Though not as hot as habanero peppers, they are definitely up there on the heat scale. What's nice about this combination is you can use the peppers as well as the sherry, depending on the demands of your particular recipe. The sherry, by the way, is definitely not for drinking straight since it's liable to set your entire digestive system on fire.

1 cup fresh Thai bird peppers (available in Asian groceries)
1 bottle dry cocktail sherry

Wash and dry the peppers. With a fork, pierce each pepper in several places. Pour off about 1 cup of sherry and reserve. Add the peppers to the remaining sherry and pour back as much of the reserved sherry as will fit. Replace the cork and store the sherry in a cool, dark place for 2 weeks before using. Leave the peppers in the sherry except for those you choose to use in a recipe.

Five Spice Sherry

Because of the number and quantity of flavoring ingredients in this recipe, it's best to make it in a large, wide-mouth jar. The five spices used in this recipe are a classic Chinese combination.

¼ cup Szechwan peppercorns
¼ cup star anise
¼ cup fennel seed
¼ cup whole cloves
Four 2- to 3-inch sticks cinnamon
1 bottle dry cocktail sherry

Place all the spices in a wide-mouth jar. Pour in the sherry. Cover and store in a cool, dark place for 2 weeks. Strain the sherry through several layers of cheesecloth back into the original bottle.

Fruited Sherries

Lots of different fruits are just the ticket for flavoring sherry. And what's great about using fruits to flavor sherry is that after they've done their job, they are eminently edible (and delicious!).

Some fruits, alone or in combination, that are perfect for flavoring sherry include pears, peaches, plums, and citrus (lemons, limes, oranges). Use about 2 cups of cored, seeded, and diced fruit for 1 bottle of sherry. When making citrus-flavored sherries, use the peel from 4 to 5 fruits and replace about ¼ cup of the sherry with freshly squeezed fruit juice.

The method for making fruited sherries is the same as for making other sherries. Use a wide-mouth jar, allow the flavoring ingredients to steep in the sherry for 2 weeks before straining and bottling, and, of course, store in a cool, dark place.

Experiment using dry cocktail sherries as well as the sweeter varieties. Sweeter fruits will, naturally, yield a sweeter finished product.

Ginger Sherry

An old Chinese trick for preserving fresh ginger is to peel, chop, or grate fresh ginger, put it in a jar, and cover it with dry sherry or Chinese wine.

One 4- to 5-inch piece fresh ginger
1 bottle dry cocktail sherry

Peel the ginger and coarsely chop or grate it into a wide-mouth jar. Pour the sherry into the jar, cover, and store in a cool, dark place for 2 weeks. Strain the sherry through several layers of cheesecloth into the original bottle. Save the ginger in a small jar or bottle with just enough sherry to cover and refrigerate. Use this in any recipe calling for fresh ginger.

Ginger Garlic Sherry

Ginger and garlic are a classic oriental combination. As with simple ginger sherry, the flavoring ingredients can be saved for cooking purposes after they have done their job.

One 4- to 5-inch piece fresh ginger
1 head garlic
1 bottle dry cocktail sherry

Peel and coarsely chop or grate the ginger into a wide-mouth bottle. Separate the head of garlic into individual cloves, crush them slightly with the flat side of a knife, and peel them. Add the garlic to the bottle. Pour the sherry into the bottle, cover, and store in a cool, dark place for 2 weeks. Strain the sherry into the original bottle and replace the cork. Reserve the garlic and ginger in a small jar with just enough sherry to cover and refrigerate. Use in any recipe calling for fresh ginger and garlic.

Ginger and Red Pepper Sherry

This combination will come in handy in many Caribbean and oriental recipes. It packs heat as well as flavor.

One 4- to 5-inch piece fresh ginger
1 cup whole fresh, ripe, red chili peppers, such
   as cayenne or serrano
1 bottle dry cocktail sherry

Peel the ginger and coarsely chop or grate it into a wide-mouth jar. Wash and dry the peppers. Pierce them in several places with a fork or knife and add them to the jar. Pour the sherry into the jar, cover, and store in a cool, dark place for 2 weeks. Put 1 or 2 fresh chilies into the original sherry bottle. Strain the sherry through several layers of cheesecloth into the bottle. Reserve the ginger and chili peppers in a small jar with just enough sherry to cover and refrigerate. Use in any recipes calling for fresh ginger or hot peppers.

Jalapeño Sherry

What's great about this sherry is that you not only end up with lots of hot jalapeño-flavored sherry, but you also have a lot of sherry-flavored jalapeños that can be used in recipes calling for hot peppers, or, better yet (if you dare), just eaten out of hand. Devilishly hot but very delicious! Leave the jalapeños in the sherry until you're ready to use them.

10 to 12 fresh jalapeño peppers
1 bottle dry cocktail sherry

Wash and dry the peppers. Pierce them in

several places with a fork or knife. Put them in a wide-mouth jar. Add the sherry, cover, and store in a cool, dark place for 2 weeks before using.

Jamaican Hot Pepper Sherry

Bermudian and Jamaican pepper sauces are famous for adding flavor as well as heat to any recipe in which they are used. How hot and flavorful they are depends on the variety of peppers used. This recipe calls for habanero peppers, which are considered to be the hottest in the world. They also have a very distinctive flavor all their own. Be careful when using this sherry in a recipe; a little goes a long way because of its incendiary heat.

6 to 8 fresh green, yellow, or red habanero
  peppers
4 to 5 cloves garlic, peeled and crushed
1 tablespoon whole black peppercorns
1 bottle dry cocktail sherry

Wash and dry the peppers. Pierce them in several places with a fork or knife and put them in a wide-mouth jar. Add the garlic and peppercorns. Add the sherry, cover, and store in a cool, dark place for 2 weeks. Strain the sherry through several layers of cheese-cloth into the original bottle. Discard the peppercorns but reserve the garlic and habaneros in a small jar with just enough sherry to cover and refrigerate and use in any appropriate recipes.

Lemon Mint Sherry

This is a "cool" flavor combo which lends it-self to a wide variety of uses. Simply poured over fresh fruit or sorbet, it adds a new di-mension to those foods.

2 lemons
1 cup fresh mint leaves (any variety)
1 bottle sweeter variety sherry

Wash the lemons in a mild dish detergent and warm water. Rinse well, dry, and remove all the peel. Place the peel in a wide-mouth jar. Squeeze the juice from the lemons and strain it through several layers of cheese-cloth into the jar. Wash the mint, pat it dry, and add it to the jar. Add the sherry, cover, and store in a cool, dark place for 2 weeks. Strain the sherry through several layers of cheesecloth into the original bottle. (There will be a little leftover because of the added lemon juice. Taste it; it's good!)

Rose Petal and Lime Sherry

Use a very fine sherry for this recipe because the flavors are very delicate. The rose petals also tend to give the sherry a very pretty pink hue. Make sure the rose petals are from organically grown roses to avoid any pesti-cide contamination.

1 cup red rose petals
2 limes
¼ cup sugar
1 bottle dry cocktail sherry

Wash the rose petals, dry thoroughly, and place them in a wide-mouth jar. Wash the

limes in a mild detergent and warm water. Rinse thoroughly. Peel them, adding the peels to the jar. Squeeze the juice from the limes and add it to the jar. Add the sugar. Add the sherry and stir to dissolve the sugar. Cover and store in a cool, dark place for 2 weeks. Strain the sherry through several layers of cheesecloth into the original bottle and discard the flavoring ingredients. (There will be a little sherry leftover because of the added lime juice.)

Szechwan Sherry

Anything Szechwan implies heat and pungent flavor. This recipe is no exception.

½ cup crushed dried red peppers
One 3- to 4-inch piece fresh ginger
¼ cup Szechwan peppercorns
¼ cup fennel seed
1 head garlic
1 bottle dry cocktail sherry

Add the red peppers to a wide-mouth jar. Peel the ginger and coarsely chop or grate it into the jar. Add the Szechwan peppercorns and fennel seed. Separate the head of garlic into individual cloves, crush them slightly with the flat side of a knife, and peel them. Add them to the jar. Add the sherry, cover, and store in a cool, dark place for 2 weeks. Strain the sherry through several layers of cheesecloth into the original bottle.

Vanilla Sherry

This sherry is excellent in dessert recipes, as well as simply poured over vanilla ice cream.

4 to 5 pieces vanilla bean
1 bottle plus 1 cup sweet variety sherry

Put the pieces of vanilla in a small saucepan. Add 1 cup of sherry and bring to a boil. Reduce the heat and simmer gently until the liquid is reduced by two thirds. Cool to room temperature. Add the reduced liquid and pieces of vanilla to a wide-mouth jar. Add as much sherry from the bottle as will fit. Cover and store in a cool, dark place for 2 weeks. Remove the pieces of vanilla. Place 1 piece in the original sherry bottle. Pour as much sherry as will fit into the bottle and replace the cork. Store in a cool, dark place.

PART TWO

Using Flavored Oils, Vinegars, and Sherries

Most of us today are concerned about eating healthier foods, with less fat, cholesterol, and salt. The infusions in this book are precisely what it takes to make what the doctor and the nutritionist ordered not only palatable, but a meal to look forward to.

We've known for a long time that when you take the fat and salt, or most of it at least, out of a recipe, terrible things can happen to the taste. Part of the reason for this is that we are creatures of habit. If something is supposed to have a salty bite to it, then it better well have it or it tastes flat.

The same can be said for fat. If you take all the fat out of some recipes that ordinarily are quite fatty, bizarre things happen when the food encounters our taste buds. This is in part due to the fact that some fats have a distinct and unique flavor of their own. But it also partly due to the fact that fat is largely responsible for a sensation known as "mouth-feel."

The infusions we have been making cannot substitute for all the sodium or fat in a recipe. But if you want to cut down on those ingredients, then a splash of flavored oil, vinegar, or sherry may just be what's required to lift a dish from the healthy but boring eating category to the healthy and divinely delicious column.

CHAPTER FOUR

Soups, Salads, and Appetizers

Soups and appetizers are logical candidates for using our flavored infusions. Take a handful of ordinary, mundane ingredients and add a splash of flavored oil, vinegar, or sherry and suddenly the ordinary becomes the extraordinary. The dishes that follow are guaranteed to get any meal off to an exciting, palette-awakening start.

Crab and Shrimp Bisque

A traditional bisque is a calorie- and cholesterol-laden affair that owes its richness to a base of heavy cream. This recipe duplicates the smoothness of a traditional bisque but comes in on the healthy side of good eating.

2 tablespoons butter
¼ cup finely chopped carrot
¼ cup finely chopped celery
1 cup finely chopped onion
⅓ cup all-purpose flour
1 ½ cups chicken stock
2 cups milk
1 teaspoon freshly ground black pepper
1 teaspoon lemon-pepper seasoning
1 tablespoon paprika
Salt to taste
One 16½-ounce can fancy lump crabmeat, drained
1 pound fresh medium-size shrimp, peeled and deveined
½ cup Allspice-flavored Sherry (page 37)
¼ cup finely minced fresh parsley

Melt the butter or margarine in a large deep skillet over medium heat and sauté the carrot, celery, and onion until the vegetables are soft and translucent, about 5 to 6 minutes. Add the flour, stirring to blend. Add the chicken stock, stirring, until incorporated. Add the milk, stirring, until the mixture thickens and is bubbling. Add the black pepper, lemon pepper, paprika, and salt, and stir. Add the crabmeat and shrimp. Stir, and continue to cook over medium heat until the shrimp are pink, about 4 to 6 minutes. Add the sherry, stir and cook 1 to 2 minutes longer. Ladle into serving bowls and sprinkle the parsley on top.

SERVES 4 TO 6

Shrimp and Avocado Soup

This delightful soup makes the perfect first course for an elegant dinner party. It could also be served chilled as a luncheon entrée.

1 pound medium to large shrimp
1 tablespoon Curry Oil (page 20)
2 cups chicken stock
2 scallions, cut into 1-inch pieces
2 cloves garlic, peeled and minced
¼ cup Lemon Mint Sherry (page 41)
2 teaspoons lime juice
2 large avocados, peeled, pitted, and cut into chunks
1 cup plain low-fat yogurt
¼ cup chopped cilantro (fresh coriander)

Peel and devein the shrimp and cut in half lengthwise. Reserve the shells. Heat the curry oil in a saucepan over medium-high heat and add the shrimp shells. Sauté until the shells turn red, about 3 to 4 minutes. Discard the shells. Add the shrimp to the saucepan and sauté until they turn pink, about 3 to 4 minutes. Remove the shrimp from the saucepan, drain, and keep warm.

Add the remaining ingredients except the yogurt and the cilantro. Cook, stirring, over medium-high heat until the mixture bubbles. Pour the mixture into a food processor and process until smooth. Pour the mixture back into the saucepan and blend in the yogurt, add the shrimp, and heat through. Ladle the soup into serving bowls and garnish with the cilantro.

SERVES 4

Eggplant and Zucchini Soup

Here's another way to get rid of the zucchini that becomes ubiquitous as summer heats up. Serve this soup either warm or at room temperature.

¼ cup Provençal Oil (page 22)
1 large sweet white onion, coarsely chopped
2 to 3 cloves garlic, minced
12 ounces fresh mushrooms, sliced
1 medium-size zucchini cut into ½-inch dice
1 medium-size eggplant cut into ½-inch dice
2 cups coarsely chopped plum tomatoes
4 cups chicken stock, preferably homemade
1 teaspoon dried oregano
1 teaspoon dried basil
1 teaspoon dried thyme
½ teaspoon crushed dried red peppers
Salt and freshly ground black pepper to taste
½ cup Lemon Mint Sherry (page 41)
¼ cup fresh mint, minced

Heat the oil in a large pot over medium-high heat. Add the onion and garlic and sauté until the vegetables are wilted. Add the mushrooms and sauté until they give up their liquid, about 5 to 6 minutes. Add the zucchini, eggplant, and tomatoes and sauté 2 to 3 minutes. Add the chicken stock, oregano, basil, thyme, and red pepper. Bring to a boil, reduce heat, and simmer for approximately 45 minutes.

Add salt and pepper to taste. Stir in the sherry, remove from the heat, and serve. Garnish each serving with some of the mint leaves.

SERVES 4 TO 6

Lemon Broccoli Soup

Lemon and broccoli seem a natural go-together. This is another soup you can serve warm or cool, depending on your mood. Served cool it is a perfect first course for an al fresco light summer supper.

2 tablespoons Lemon Thyme Oil (page 22)
1 large sweet white onion, coarsely chopped
1 bunch fresh broccoli, including stems, coarsely chopped
¼ cup freshly squeezed lemon juice
4 cups chicken stock, preferably homemade
8 ounces plain low-fat yogurt
1 tablespoon cornstarch
¼ cup Lemon Mint Sherry (page 41)
Salt and freshly ground black pepper to taste
¼ cup minced cilantro (fresh coriander)

Heat the lemon thyme oil in a soup pot over medium heat. Add the onion and sauté until wilted, about 5 to 6 minutes. Add the broccoli and lemon juice and sauté until the broccoli softens, about 3 to 4 minutes. Add the chicken stock, bring to a boil, reduce the heat, and simmer gently for 25 to 30 minutes.

Puree the soup in a blender or food processor. Return it to the pot and stirring, over low heat, add the yogurt. Separately, combine the cornstarch and sherry, and add it to the soup. Bring the soup back to a simmer and cook for 8 to 10 minutes. The soup may be served at this point or cooled and served later. In either case, garnish with the cilantro just before serving.

SERVES 6

Hot-and-sour Soup with Hot Pepper Sherry

This recipe is sort of an east meets west version of hot and sour soup. It starts out traditionally enough, using a base of chicken stock and building from there. But things take an interesting twist when we spritz a little Jamaican Hot Pepper Sherry in it.

½ pound small fresh shrimp, peeled and de-veined, shells reserved
1 tablespoon Chili Pepper Oil (page 19)
4 cups chicken stock
4 to 5 fresh chili peppers, such as serrano
2 to 3 stalks cilantro (fresh coriander), roots finely chopped, leaves shredded
1 stalk lemon grass, bottom part only, finely minced
¼ cup fresh lime juice
8 ounces fresh mushrooms, sliced
1 tablespoon Thai fish sauce (available in Asian groceries)
¼ cup Jamaican Hot Pepper Sherry (page 41)

Heat a wok over high heat and add the oil. When the oil is almost smoking, add the reserved shrimp shells and stir-fry them until they are red. Using a strainer, strain shells, returning the oil to the wok.

Add the chicken stock, bring it to a boil, reduce the heat, and simmer. Add the chilies, cilantro roots, half the shredded cilantro leaves, lemon grass, lime juice, and mushrooms. Simmer 6 to 8 minutes. Add the fish sauce and the shrimp. Simmer 2 minutes. Turn off the heat and let the soup stand for 5 to 6 minutes. Add the sherry, garnish with the remaining cilantro leaves, and serve.

SERVES 4

Garlic Soup

Garlic soup is a staple in the Spanish-speaking world. It comes in many guises but no matter what recipe you may encounter, you can rest assured of one thing: there's bound to plenty of garlic in it.

¼ cup Ginger Spice Oil (page 21)
1 head garlic, separated into individual cloves, peeled, and minced
1 tablespoon paprika
1 teaspoon cayenne pepper
4 slices day-old bread, cubed
4 cups chicken stock
Salt and freshly ground black pepper to taste
4 eggs, well beaten

Heat the oil in a skillet or wok over medium heat. Add the garlic and sauté until softened but not browned. Add the paprika, cayenne, and bread cubes. Sauté until the bread cubes are browned and crisp. Add the chicken stock, salt, and pepper and bring to a boil. Reduce heat and simmer gently for 35 to 45 minutes.

Increase the heat slightly so the soup is just gently bubbling and add the eggs, stirring constantly, to make the eggs "thread" as they cook. Serve.

SERVES 4

Burmese Squash Soup

This is a hearty soup that will warm your tummy and your soul on a cold winter's evening.

2 tablespoons Curry Oil (page 20)
8 ounces small to medium shrimp, peeled, deveined, and coarsely chopped
1 medium-size onion, peeled and coarsely chopped
1 teaspoon finely minced fresh garlic
2 to 3 fresh, hot red chili peppers, such as serrano
6 cups chicken stock
2 teaspoons fish sauce (available in Asian groceries)
5 cups winter squash, peeled, seeded, and cubed

Heat the oil in a soup pot or wok over medium-high heat and add the shrimp. Stir-fry the shrimp until they turn pink. Remove them with a slotted spoon and set aside. Add the onion, garlic, and chili peppers to the wok. Stir-fry until the onion is translucent, about 4 to 5 minutes. Add the chicken stock, fish sauce, and squash cubes. Bring to a boil, reduce the heat, and simmer 25 to 30 minutes, or until the squash is tender.

Process the soup in a food processor or blender until smooth. Return the soup to the wok and add the shrimp. Warm through, about 3 to 4 minutes, and serve.

SERVES 4 TO 6

Chinese Clam and Shrimp Soup

This is a simple soup that could be included as part of an oriental dinner. You can make it ahead of time and refrigerate it, rewarming it just before serving. If you choose this route then omit the cilantro and sherry until just before serving.

2 teaspoons Curry Oil (page 20)
1 small onion, peeled and finely chopped
3 dozen littleneck clams
3 cups bottled clam juice
3 cups chicken stock
2 tablespoons soy sauce
1 pound medium-size shrimp, peeled, deveined, and cut in half lengthwise
¼ cup Ginger and Red Pepper Sherry (page 39)
3 tablespoons minced cilantro (fresh coriander)

Heat the curry oil in a wok or stockpot over medium heat. Add the onion and sauté 2 to 3 minutes. Add the clams, cover tightly, and cook over medium heat until the clams open, about 5 to 7 minutes. Discard any clams that do not open. Remove the clams with a slotted spoon, remove them from the shells, and discard the shells.

Add the clam juice, chicken stock, and soy sauce to the pot. Bring to a boil, add the shrimp, reduce the heat, and simmer gently 5 to 7 minutes, or until the shrimp are pink. Return the clams to the soup. Stir in the sherry and cilantro and serve.

SERVES 6 TO 8

Thai-style Vegetable Curry Soup

This is a spicy soup that will make the sweat beads pop out on your forehead so be forewarned. Prepare the yellow curry paste before making the soup.

FOR THE YELLOW CURRY PASTE:

3 to 4 fresh, hot red or green chili peppers, such as serrano or Thai bird peppers
2 tablespoons finely minced shallots
2 tablespoons finely minced garlic
1 stalk lemon grass, bottom part only, finely minced (available in Asian groceries)
1 tablespoon grated galangal (available in Asian groceries, or use freshly grated ginger)
2 teaspoons ground coriander
2 teaspoons ground cumin
1 teaspoon turmeric
½ teaspoon ground cloves
1 teaspoon freshly ground white pepper
1 tablespoon shrimp or anchovy paste
1 teaspoon salt

FOR THE SOUP:

2 tablespoons Curry Oil (page 20)
1 large onion, peeled and finely chopped
2 teaspoons finely minced garlic
5 cups chicken stock
1 cup coconut milk
¼ cup Thai yellow curry paste
1 medium-size zucchini, cut into ½-inch dice
1 medium-size carrot, scraped and cut into ¼-inch dice
2 potatoes, scrubbed but unpeeled, cut into ½-inch dice
1 red bell pepper, cored, seeded, and cut into ½-inch pieces
1 cup shredded cabbage
2 large tomatoes, cored, seeds pressed out, and diced
¼ cup Ginger and Red Pepper Sherry (page 39)
¼ cup minced cilantro (fresh coriander)

In a food processor process the chili peppers, shallots, garlic, lemon grass, galangal, coriander, cumin, cloves, and white pepper. Process very fine. Put the spice mixture in a mixing bowl and mix in the shrimp paste and salt. Add a few drops of water if necessary to make the mixture form a paste.

In a wok or stockpot heat the oil over medium-high heat and stir-fry the onion and garlic 2 to 3 minutes. Add the chicken stock, coconut milk, and curry paste. Bring the mixture to a boil and add the zucchini, carrot, potatoes, red bell pepper, cabbage, and tomatoes. Reduce the heat and simmer 20 to 25 minutes, or until the vegetables are tender. Stir in the sherry and cilantro and serve.

SERVES 6 TO 8

Shrimp, Crab, and Corn Soup

This soup has definite Chinese roots but needn't be confined to an oriental meal. It's good enough to be the first course for any meal. It's also quick and simple to make.

Two 8-ounce cans crabmeat, drained and picked over or substitute an equal amount of imitation crabmeat
1 pound small to medium shrimp, peeled, deveined, and butterflied
One 16-ounce can creamed corn
5 cups chicken stock
1 tablespoon cornstarch
1 cup Ginger Garlic Sherry (page 39)
Freshly ground white pepper to taste

In a saucepan combine the crabmeat, shrimp, creamed corn, and chicken stock. Bring the mixture to a boil, reduce the heat,

and simmer gently 6 to 8 minutes. Mix the cornstarch with the sherry and add it to the soup. Cook over medium heat, stirring, until the soup thickens, about 3 to 4 minutes. Add white pepper to taste and serve.

SERVES 4 TO 6

Cold Broiled Tuna Salad

Fresh tuna is a delicious, firm-textured fish that takes well to a variety of treatments. This recipe makes an excellent light supper entrée, needing only some crusty French bread and a chilled white wine to round out the meal.

1 pound fresh tuna steaks, cut 1 inch thick
¼ cup Rice Wine Vinegar with Shallots and Herbs (page 34)
¼ cup Sesame Oil with Szechwan Peppercorns (page 23)
4 cups mixed salad greens, such as Boston, endive, and red or green leaf lettuce
1 small red onion, thinly sliced and separated into rings
½ cup shredded carrot
2 cups new red potatoes, unpeeled, cooked, drained, and cut into 1-inch pieces

Place the tuna steaks in a baking dish and pour 2 tablespoons of the vinegar and 2 tablespoons of the sesame oil over them. Marinate at room temperature for 20 minutes, or 1 hour under refrigeration. Broil or grill the steaks until just barely done in the center, about 4 minutes on each side. Cool and slice thinly.

Divide the salad greens among four serving plates. Add one fourth of the onion, carrot, and potatoes to each plate. Divide the

tuna slices among the four plates. Mix the remaining vinegar and oil and dribble an equal amount over each salad.

SERVES 4

Orange Salad with Black Olives and Capers

This salad is typically Mediterranean. It is the perfect summer salad when dining al fresco.

4 large navel oranges
2 tablespoons capers, rinsed
½ cup pitted and coarsely chopped oil-cured black olives
½ cup Rice Wine Vinegar with Garlic (page 33)
½ cup Green Herb Oil (page 21)
¼ cup chopped fresh parsley

Peel and section the oranges. Remove as much of the white pith as possible. In a bowl, toss the orange sections, capers, and black olives. Whisk the vinegar and oil together and pour over the oranges. Add the parsley and toss to coat everything evenly. Refrigerate for several hours before serving.

SERVES 4

Shrimp and Snow Pea Salad

This salad can actually be the main dish for a light summer luncheon or late-night supper. You can assemble it ahead of time and refrigerate it until you're ready to serve it, but don't add the dressing until just before serving.

Orange Salad with Black Olives and Capers

1 pound medium-size shrimp, peeled and deveined
1 cup fresh snow peas
1 pound fresh spinach leaves
4 ounces fresh mushrooms, sliced
¼ cup Tarragon Dill Vinegar (page 35)
¼ cup Dijon-style mustard
1 teaspoon freshly ground black pepper
½ cup Oil with Fines Herbes (page 21)

Cook the shrimp in boiling water for 4 to 5 minutes, or until just cooked. Drain and cool. Blanch the snow peas in boiling water for 30 seconds. Immediately plunge them into ice water. Drain them in a colander.

Wash and dry the spinach leaves. Tear them coarsely and divide them among four salad plates. Divide the shrimp, snow peas, and mushrooms among the four plates. In a bowl, whisk together the vinegar, mustard, and pepper. Slowly add the oil in a very thin stream, whisking constantly. Pour the dressing over the salads and serve.

SERVES 4

Spinach, Grapefruit, and Avocado Salad

This is another quick, easy to prepare salad that makes an excellent side dish for a light summer supper.

1 pound fresh spinach
8 ounces fresh mushrooms, thinly sliced
1 pink grapefruit
1 avocado
1 tablespoon lime juice

1 tablespoon sugar

¼ cup Raspberry Lemon Vinegar (page 33)

2 tablespoons Allspice and Bay Oil (page 17)

Wash and dry the spinach. Tear up the leaves and spread them on a large serving platter. Distribute the mushrooms evenly on top of the spinach. Peel and section the grapefruit. Try to remove all the white pith. Halve the sections and distribute them evenly over the spinach and mushrooms.

Peel and pit the avocado. Cut it into slices and quickly toss it with the lime juice to prevent it from browning. Layer it on top of the other ingredients. Dissolve the sugar in the vinegar. Mix the vinegar with the oil and pour it evenly over all.

SERVES 4

Asparagus Salad with Orange Pistachio Sauce

Asparagus is a lovely vegetable that most people associate with springtime. Thanks to modern transportation, however, it is now available year-round (if you're willing to pay for it). Simply steamed and drizzled with butter is definitely the best way to serve the first young, tender shoots of the season, but this recipe is delicious and perfect for those less slender stalks of early summer.

1 pound asparagus

1 small red onion

1 red bell pepper

6 tablespoons (¾ stick) butter

¼ cup crushed pistachio nuts

¼ cup Lemon Mint Sherry (page 41)

2 tablespoons orange juice concentrate

Grated zest of 1 orange

Freshly ground black pepper to taste

Cut the asparagus into 1-inch pieces and steam until just crisp-tender, 4 to 5 minutes. Plunge the asparagus into ice water for a few seconds to stop it from cooking and to set the color. Slice the red onion in half lengthwise and then slice into thin strips. Seed and core the red pepper and slice it into thin strips.

In a mixing bowl, toss the asparagus, onion, and pepper. In a saucepan, melt the butter over medium heat and add the remaining ingredients. Stir constantly 3 to 4 minutes. Pour the sauce over the asparagus and serve.

SERVES 4

Corn and Black Bean Salad

This salad has a decidedly Caribbean flair to it. It is good served at room temperature or chilled, and makes a wonderful addition to a picnic lunch. The frozen corn kernels are blanched in processing so only need to be thawed and drained.

1 medium-size head romaine lettuce, torn into bite-sized pieces

4 cups frozen whole-kernel corn, thawed and drained

Two 16-ounce cans black beans, rinsed and drained

1 red bell pepper, cored, seeded, and cut into ½-inch dice

1 red onion, peeled and cut into ¼-inch dice

2 habanero or serrano peppers, seeded and finely diced

3 tablespoons Ginger Spice Oil (page 21)

2 tablespoons Ginger Garlic Vinegar (page 29)

1 teaspoon freshly ground black pepper

½ teaspoon crushed dried red pepper

¼ cup chopped cilantro (fresh coriander)

Salt to taste

12 cherry tomatoes

Spread the romaine evenly on a large serving platter. Mix together the corn, beans, bell pepper, onion, and chili peppers. Mound the mixture over the romaine, leaving a green border all around.

Mix together the oil, vinegar, black pepper, red pepper, cilantro, and salt. Pour over the beans and corn. Garnish with the cherry tomatoes and serve.

SERVES 6

Jamaican Shrimp Salad

Jamaica. Bright sun. White sand. Blue skies. Crystal clear ocean. Cold rum concoctions. And shrimp. And . . . culinary heat. This dish is perfect for an al fresco lunch or supper on a warm summer's day as it's hearty enough to serve as an entrée. Be sure you have plenty of ice-cold beer or your favorite rum drink on hand. You'll need it to put out the flames!

1 pound medium to large shrimp, peeled, deveined, and butterflied

One 10-ounce package fresh spinach, washed and dried well

1 small head romaine lettuce torn into bite-size pieces

8 ounces fresh mushrooms, sliced

1 red bell pepper, cored, seeded, and cut into strips

1 habanero or serrano pepper, seeded and diced

2 scallions cut into 1-inch pieces

2 tablespoons Ginger Spice Oil (page 21)

2 tablespoons Rice Wine Vinegar with Lemon Grass and Kaffir Lime (page 33)

1 tablespoon soy sauce

1 tablespoon Jamaican Hot Pepper Sherry (page 41)

2 tablespoons chopped cilantro (fresh coriander)

In a 3-quart saucepot bring 2 quarts of water to a boil. Add the shrimp and cook just until they turn opaque, about 3 minutes. Drain and chill the shrimp.

Mix the spinach, romaine, mushrooms, peppers, and scallions in a salad bowl. Add the shrimp and toss. Mix the oil, vinegar, soy sauce, and sherry and pour it over the salad and toss. Sprinkle the cilantro on top and serve.

SERVES 4

Mediterranean-style Tomato and Onion Salad

Tomatoes, onions, and black olives are staples in Mediterranean cooking. Try this salad as an addition to a light summer evening supper on the patio or at a picnic.

1 head leaf lettuce, leaves separated

4 ripe tomatoes, cored and sliced ¼ inch thick

1 small red onion, peeled and thinly sliced

½ cup oil-cured or Kalamata olives, pitted and coarsely chopped

1 cup feta cheese, crumbled

1 tablespoon shallots, finely minced

1 teaspoon Dijon-style mustard

1 teaspoon freshly ground black pepper

¼ cup Garlic Basil Vinegar (page 29)

¾ cup Provençal Oil (page 22)

Arrange the lettuce leaves on a serving platter. Layer the tomato slices evenly over the lettuce. Layer the onion slices over the tomatoes. Sprinkle the olives and feta evenly over all.

Combine all of the remaining ingredients in a bowl and drizzle over all and serve.

SERVES 4

Asparagus Salad with Lemon Thyme Vinaigrette

This is another excellent salad to accompany a light supper. It can be prepared ahead of time and dressed just before serving.

1 pound fresh asparagus cut into 1-inch pieces

1 red bell pepper, cored, seeded, and diced

1 clove garlic, finely minced

1 small serrano pepper, seeded and finely minced

1 small red onion, peeled and diced

¼ cup Rice Wine Vinegar with Lemon Grass and Kaffir Lime (page 33)

½ teaspoon freshly ground black pepper

¼ cup Lemon Thyme Oil (page 22)

Bring a pot of water to a boil. Drop in the asparagus and cook exactly 1 minute. Remove the asparagus from the boiling water and plunge it into a bowl of ice water to stop the

cooking process and set the color. Drain well.

In a salad bowl combine the asparagus, bell pepper, garlic, chili, and onion. In a mixing bowl whisk together the vinaigrette ingredients and pour over the salad just before serving.

SERVES 4

Avocado Salad with Oranges, Pistachios, and Basil

Avocados have a natural affinity for citrus fruit. Their rich, creamy, buttery texture is the perfect foil for the tart sweetness of citrus. This recipe is quick, easy, and simply delicious.

2 navel or Valencia oranges, peeled, pithed, and sectioned

2 Florida avocados, peeled, pitted, and sliced lengthwise

2 tablespoons lemon juice

½ cup (approximately) pitted and coarsely chopped Kalamata or other cured black olives

1 small red onion, peeled and cut into strips lengthwise

½ cup shredded fresh basil leaves

2 teaspoons Dijon-style mustard

2 tablespoons Garlic Basil Vinegar (page 29)

¼ cup Green Herb Oil (page 21)

Salt and freshly ground black pepper to taste

Arrange the orange sections on each of four individual salad plates. Toss the avocado slices with the lemon juice to prevent discoloration. (The avocados shouldn't be sliced too far ahead of time as they will eventually discolor even though they have been bathed in lemon juice.) Arrange the avocado slices among the orange sections. Distribute the onion strips evenly over all and sprinkle the chopped olives evenly on top. Top with the basil leaves.

In a mixing bowl combine the remaining ingredients and whisk to blend. Drizzle the dressing over all and serve.

SERVES 4

Shrimp and Avocado Salad

Avocados are versatile because they marry well with many different kinds of ingredients. Probably the most common use for avocados is in the ubiquitous guacamole dip. If you don't try them some other way, however, you're not enjoying their true potential.

24 large shrimp, about 1 pound
2 Hass avocados
1 tablespoon lemon juice
¼ cup mayonnaise
2 tablespoons chunky salsa or to taste
1 tablespoon Ground Hot Pepper Vinegar (page 29)
2 tablespoons minced cilantro (fresh coriander)
Salt and freshly ground black pepper to taste
Lettuce leaves for garnish

Peel the shrimp, leaving the last tail segment intact. Bring a pot of water to a boil, add the shrimp, and as soon as the water returns to a boil turn off the heat. Let the shrimp sit in the hot water until they are completely opaque, about 2 to 3 minutes. Drain the shrimp and chill.

Cut around each avocado lengthwise, remove the pit and scrape out the flesh into a mixing bowl. Brush the lemon juice inside each avocado shell to prevent discoloration. Add the remaining ingredients except the lettuce leaves and mix well.

Arrange the lettuce leaves on four small serving dishes or ramekins. Spoon an equal amount of the avocado mixture into each shell. Place the shells on the lettuce leaves. Place six shrimp around the edge of each shell and serve. (This can be prepared several hours ahead of time and refrigerated).

SERVES 4

Tomato, Basil, and Mozzarella Salad

This simple salad is a summer favorite around our house. In fact, this salad *is* summer. Don't even think about making this recipe unless you have tomatoes at the absolute peak of ripeness, the freshest basil, and, preferably, fresh mozzarella. Freshly made mozzarella has a milder flavor than the prepackaged variety and its texture is softer.

4 large, ripe tomatoes or 12 Italian plum tomatoes
1 red onion, peeled
8 ounces mozzarella cheese, preferably fresh
½ cup fresh basil leaves
½ cup Provençal or Thyme Oil (page 23)
Salt and freshly ground black pepper to taste

Slice the tomatoes about ¼ inch thick and layer them in a shallow baking dish or on a serving platter. Slice the red onion into

⅛-inch thick slices. Separate the slices into rings and arrange them on the tomatoes. Slice the mozzarella into ⅛-inch thick slices and arrange them on top of the onion. Shred the basil leaves and sprinkle them evenly over the salad. Pour the oil over all, add salt and pepper, and allow to sit about 30 minutes before serving.

SERVES 4

Salad of Mixed Greens and Mandarin Oranges with Sun–dried Tomato Vinaigrette

Sun-dried tomatoes are turning up in the strangest places. Originally a novelty and mostly in the sole purvey of upscale restaurants, sun-dried tomatoes are available virtually everywhere now, and if for some strange reason you can't find them you can always make your own.

4 to 6 cups mixed salad greens, such as bib, romaine, green and red leaf lettuce, curly endive, radicchio, etc.
1 small red onion, peeled, root end cut off, and sliced vertically into strips
1 red bell pepper, cored, seeded, and cut into strips
½ cup oil-cured black olives, pitted
1 small can mandarin orange segments, packed in syrup, drained, syrup reserved
1 cup (approximately) red, ripe cherry tomatoes
½ cup Garlic Basil Vinegar (page 29)
¼ cup Ginger Garlic Sherry (page 39)
¼ cup tomato paste
Reserved mandarin orange syrup

1 teaspoon minced garlic
2 tablespoons grated white onion
½ teaspoon dried oregano
½ teaspoon dried basil
½ teaspoon dried thyme
½ teaspoon salt
½ teaspoon freshly ground black pepper
½ teaspoon crushed dried red pepper
1 cup Pizza or Provençal Oil (page 22)
½ cup minced oil-packed sun-dried tomatoes

Arrange the greens on a large serving platter. Distribute the onion, bell pepper, olives, orange segments, and cherry tomatoes evenly and decoratively over the greens.

In a blender or food processor combine all the remaining ingredients except the oil and sun-dried tomatoes. Process until smooth. With the processor running, add the oil in a steady stream until it has all been incorporated. Add the sun-dried tomatoes and process just until the tomatoes are mixed through. Pour the vinaigrette over the salad and serve.

SERVES 4 TO 6

Squid Salad

Squid is not nearly as popular in this country as it is in Mediterranean and oriental cuisines. It has a mild, slightly sweet flavor that lends itself to a multitude of treatments. Squid is marketed in various forms, the least expensive being whole and uncleaned. It is not difficult to clean but for convenience whole, eviscerated bodies can't be beat. This salad makes an excellent light summer lunch entrée or a perfect dinner first course.

1 pound cleaned squid
½ cup Lemon Thyme Oil (page 22)
¼ cup Rice Wine Vinegar with Garlic (page 33)
Juice of 1 lemon
1 small red onion, finely chopped
2 teaspoons minced garlic
3 to 4 stalks celery, leaves included, finely chopped
1 teaspoon dried thyme or 2 teaspoons fresh, minched
1 teaspoon dried basil or 2 teaspoons fresh, minced
1 teaspoon dried oregano or 2 teaspoons fresh, minced
Salt and freshly ground black pepper to taste
2 tablespoons minced fresh parsley

Bring a large pot of water to a boil and add the squid. Cook just until the squid turns opaque and is firm to the touch, approximately 3 minutes. Do not overcook or the squid will get tough and chewy. Drain the squid and rinse it under cold running water to cool. Slice the bodies into ¼-inch rings. If there are tentacles, chop them.

Place the squid in a mixing bowl and add the remaining ingredients except the parsley. Cover, refrigerate, and allow to marinate several hours or overnight. Before serving, garnish with the parsley.

SERVES 4

Chicken Salad with Dijon Honey Dressing

This recipe was inspired by a meal I had at a little inn in upstate New York. The name of the place escapes me and the chef wouldn't part with the recipe anyway, so I went to the drawing board and came up with my own version. This dish is perfect as an entrée for a light summer lunch.

2 cups water
3 or 4 whole allspice berries
1 bay leaf
4 or 5 whole black peppercorns
Sprig fresh lemon thyme
Sprig fresh parsley
1 scallion, cut into 1-inch pieces
1 whole boneless, skinless chicken breast
2 apples, cored and unpeeled
1 tablespoon lemon juice
½ cup coarsely chopped walnuts
2 stalks celery, coarsely chopped
1 small red onion, peeled and diced
½ cup mayonnaise
2 tablespoons Allspice-flavored Sherry (page 37)
⅓ cup honey
2 tablespoons Dijon-style mustard
2 tablespoons minced fresh parsley

In a saucepan combine the water, allspice, bay leaf, peppercorns, thyme, parsley, scallion, and chicken breast. Bring to a boil, reduce heat, and simmer just until the chicken is cooked through, 8 to 10 minutes. Turn off the heat and allow the chicken to cool in the liquid. When it is cool, drain, pat it dry, and cut it into ½-inch cubes.

Cube the apples and toss with the lemon juice to prevent them from browning. In a mixing bowl combine the chicken, apples, walnuts, celery, and red onion. In another bowl mix together the mayonnaise, sherry, honey, and mustard. Add this to the chicken mixture and mix to coat everything thoroughly with the dressing. Transfer the salad to a serving bowl, garnish with the parsley and serve.

SERVES 4

Shrimp and Cauliflower Salad with Curried Vinaigrette

This is another quick and simple salad that can be prepared ahead of time and served cold. If you can't find fresh snow peas you can use frozen ones but only thaw them out as they were blanched before they were frozen.

2 quarts water
1 head cauliflower broken into florets
8 ounces snow peas
1 pound small to medium shrimp, peeled and deveined
¼ cup Ginger Garlic Vinegar (page 29)
¼ teaspoon ground cardamom
¼ teaspoon cayenne pepper
¼ teaspoon ground cumin
¼ teaspoon ground coriander
¼ teaspoon ground fennel seed
¼ teaspoon mace
¼ teaspoon nutmeg
¼ teaspoon freshly ground black pepper
¼ teaspoon turmeric
½ cup Curry Oil (page 20)

Bring the water to a boil, drop in the cauliflower, and cook 1 minute. Remove the cauliflower with a slotted spoon and rinse it under cold water to stop it from cooking further. Drain and put it in a mixing bowl. Drop the snow peas into the boiling water and cook 1 minute, then remove with a slotted spoon and rinse under cold water. Drain and add it to the cauliflower.

Drop the shrimp into the water, turn off the heat, and let the shrimp cook in the hot water until they are pink and opaque, 8 to 10 minutes. Remove the shrimp, rinse under cold water, drain well, and add them to the cauliflower and snow peas. In a mixing bowl combine all the remaining ingredients, mix well and pour the vinaigrette over the cauliflower, snow peas, and shrimp. Cover and refrigerate several hours or overnight.

SERVES 6 TO 8

Fennel and Radicchio Salad

Radicchio is becoming much more common in grocery stores but, alas, its price has not come down as much as one might expect. There are several varieties of radicchio but the most common, and the ones you are most likely to encounter in your local grocer's produce case, are radicchio di Verona and radicchio di Treviso. Both have pinkish to purple leaves with white ribs, making them a very colorful addition to a salad.

Bulb fennel is called Florence fennel, or *finocchio* in Italian. It shouldn't be confused with sweet anise which, though similar, has a much more licorice scent and flavor.

1 head radicchio
1 bulb fennel, thinly sliced
1 red bell pepper, cored, seeded, and cut into strips
8 ounces fresh white mushrooms, sliced
¼ cup Garlic Basil Vinegar (page 29)
2 tablespoons minced shallots
1 teaspoon freshly ground black pepper

Salt to taste
½ cup Fennel Oil (page 20)

Separate the radicchio leaves and place them on a serving platter to make a bed for the other ingredients. Arrange the fennel slices on top of the radicchio. Arrange the red pepper strips over the fennel, and finally distribute the mushrooms over the red pepper.

In a mixing bowl combine the vinegar, shallots, black pepper, salt, and oil. Pour this over the salad and serve.

SERVES 4

Tomato, Olive, and Feta Salad

This salad definitely has Greek roots. Enjoy it in the summertime when tomatoes are at their peak.

1 pound ripe tomatoes, cored and cut into ½-inch slices
1 small red onion, peeled and cut into ¼-inch slices, separated into rings
¼ cup Kalamata olives, pitted and coarsely chopped
1 cup feta cheese, crumbled
¼ cup Rice Wine Vinegar with Garlic (page 33)
2 tablespoons minced shallots
½ teaspoon thyme leaves
½ teaspoon dried oregano
Salt and freshly ground black pepper to taste
½ cup Lemon Thyme Oil (page 22)

Arrange the tomato slices on a serving platter. Arrange the onion rings over the tomatoes. Spread the olives evenly over the onions and tomatoes and finally top with the feta cheese. In a mixing bowl, combine the vinegar, shallots, thyme, oregano, salt, pepper, and oil. Pour over the salad and serve.

SERVES 4

Baby Artichokes with Garlic and Herbs

This is an interesting appetizer that can be prepared in minutes. You won't always be able to find baby artichokes in your local grocery store, but when you do, this is definitely a dish you should give a whirl.

2 dozen baby artichokes, the smaller the better
1 teaspoon finely minced garlic
1 teaspoon oregano leaves
1 teaspoon thyme leaves
½ teaspoon freshly ground black pepper
2 tablespoons Green Herb Oil (page 21)
¼ cup fresh bread crumbs
Salt to taste

Preheat the broiler. Wash the artichokes and cut off the outer leaves. Cut about ¼ inch off the top of each one. Cut each in half lengthwise. Bring a pot of water to a boil and plunge the artichokes into the water and cook just until the artichokes are crisp-tender, 2 to 3 minutes. Rinse and drain.

In a baking dish combine the artichokes, garlic, oregano, thyme, and pepper. Drizzle the oil over all and toss to coat evenly. Sprinkle the bread crumbs evenly over all, add salt to taste, and place the dish under the broiler just until the bread crumbs start to brown, about 1 minute.

SERVES 4 TO 6 AS AN APPETIZER

Pepper Shooters

There's a story behind this recipe. "Pepper shooters" are stuffed pickled hot cherry peppers. They are a favorite appetizer among the Italian population in the southern tier of New York State. Whether they in fact originated with this population or, as is quite likely, were transported there from Italy, they remain a perennial favorite among the Italian men who gather together to make wine. Wine needs to be sampled, of course, to see just how well it's doing. But if you sample enough wine without some food to go along with it, you might soon find yourself incapable of rendering any objective opinion about wine, or anything else for that matter. Tradition has it that when men gather to make, sample, and judge their homemade wines they lay in a storehouse of freshly baked Italian bread and pepper shooters to palliate the effects of the alcohol.

24 large red or green pickled hot cherry peppers
12 thin slices prosciutto
Twenty-four ¾-inch-square pieces aged provolone cheese
2 cups Pizza Oil (page 22)

Core and seed the cherry peppers, leaving the peppers whole. Slice each piece of prosciutto in half lengthwise. Place a piece of provolone cheese on each piece of prosciutto and wrap the cheese up completely. Stuff each piece of prosciutto-wrapped cheese in a cherry pepper.

Place the peppers in a shallow baking dish and pour the oil over them. The oil should just barely cover the peppers. Cover and re-frigerate overnight. The peppers will become mellower and the oil spicier the longer they marinate. Allow the peppers to come almost to room temperature before serving. (Because olive oil gets cloudy and thickens when it is refrigerated, it's important to let it warm up before serving.)

SERVES 8 AS AN APPETIZER

Sesame Stuffed Mushrooms

Stuffed mushrooms make a great appetizer or addition to the buffet table. Choose large, unblemished mushrooms for best eye appeal.

12 large fresh mushrooms
1 tablespoon Sesame Oil with Szechwan Peppercorns (page 23)
2 teaspoons minced garlic
3 tablespoons finely chopped onion
1 tablespoon Szechwan Sherry (page 43)
1 tablespoon soy sauce
2 teaspoons toasted sesame seeds
1 cup fresh bread crumbs
Salt and freshly ground black pepper to taste
2 tablespoons minced cilantro (fresh coriander)

Prehead the oven to 350°F. Remove the stems from the mushrooms, chop the stems finely, and reserve the caps. Heat the oil in a skillet or wok over medium-high heat. Add the mushroom stems, garlic, and onion. Sauté until the onion is just wilted, 2 to 3 minutes. Add the sherry, soy sauce, sesame seeds, bread crumbs, salt, and pepper and mix well.

Mound equal amounts of the stuffing mixture in each of the mushroom caps.

Spray a cookie sheet with vegetable oil and place the mushrooms on it. Cook in the preheated oven until the filling is heated through and the mushrooms are slightly browned on top, 6 to 8 minutes.

SERVES 4

Dilly Pickled Green Beans

Here's a nifty little recipe you can throw together, stick in the refrigerator, and pull out when you need one more little something on the buffet table or hors d'oeuvres tray.

1 pound fresh green beans
2 cups Tarragon Dill Vinegar (page 35)
2 cups water
2 tablespoons salt
4 cloves garlic
10 whole black peppercorns
2 whole dried red chili pepper pods

String and destem the beans if necessary. Bring a pot of water to a boil and add the beans. Cook 2 minutes and immediately plunge the beans in cold water to stop cooking. Drain. Divide the beans between two quart jars.

Mix the vinegar, water, and salt in a saucepan. Bring the liquid to a boil and add the garlic, peppercorns, and chili peppers. Pour this mixture over the beans, cover, and when the jars are cool to the touch, refrigerate them. Allow the beans to sit in the pickling liquid for at least 2 or 3 days before sampling.

2 QUARTS

Thai-style Chicken Wings with Sweet-and-Sour Chili Sauce

The Thais have a great way of preparing chicken wings. If you're an aficionado of Buffalo wings, especially if you like them suicidal on the heat scale, then this recipe is for you. If you can't find any habanero peppers feel free to substitute any hot red chili, but be forewarned that the heat will be lacking.

24 chicken wings
½ cup peanut or vegetable oil for frying
1 tablespoon Sesame Oil with Szechwan Peppercorns (page 23)
2 teaspoons minced garlic
2 teaspoons minced galangal (available in Asian groceries; if you can't find it, substitute fresh ginger)
2 habanero peppers, finely chopped, seeds included
¼ cup firmly packed brown sugar
1 cup pineapple juice
¼ cup Jamaican Hot Pepper Sherry (page 41)
¼ cup Ground Hot Pepper Vinegar (page 29)
2 teaspoons cornstarch
2 tablespoons water
3 tablespoons minced cilantro (fresh coriander)

Pat the wings dry with a paper towel so they don't splatter when fried. Heat the peanut oil in a wok and fry the wings, a few at a time, until they are crispy on the outside and cooked through. Drain them on paper towels and set aside.

Drain off all the oil in the wok and add

the Szechwan oil. Add the garlic, galangal, and habaneros to the wok and stir-fry for 1 to 2 minutes. Dissolve the brown sugar in the pineapple juice and add it to the wok. Add the sherry and vinegar. Bring to a boil. Dissolve the cornstarch in the water and add it to the wok. Cook, stirring, until the sauce thickens.

Return the wings to the wok, reduce the heat, and cook until the wings are heated through, 3 to 4 minutes. Place the wings on a serving platter, pour the sauce over them, and garnish with the cilantro.

SERVES 6 TO 8

Sherried Shrimp

This is a simple, easy to prepare hors d'oeuvre that makes an excellent prelude to light summer meal. Although you can serve this warm, it's much better chilled, especially if you make it a day or so ahead of time and allow the flavors to permeate the shrimp.

2 tablespoons Lemon Thyme Oil (page 22)
1 small onion, peeled and finely minced
2 cloves garlic, finely minced
1 cup Lemon Mint Sherry (page 41)
1 pound large shrimp, peeled and deveined, tail segment left intact
Salt and freshly ground black pepper to taste

Heat the oil in a skillet over medium heat and add the onion and garlic. Sauté until the onion is translucent, about 4 to 5 minutes. Add the sherry and bring to a boil. Add the shrimp, bring the liquid back to a boil, and

turn off the heat. Allow the shrimp to poach for 10 minutes. Chill.

SERVES 4 TO 6

Shrimp Satay

Satays are popular throughout the Pacific rim countries. They are street food popular even where McDonald's is readily available. Be sure to soak your bamboo skewers at least 45 minutes before using them to prevent their incineration when placed over hot coals.

4 tablespoons Curry Oil (page 20)
2 tablespoons finely minced garlic
1 teaspoon freshly grated ginger
1 small onion, peeled and finely minced
¼ cup peanut butter
2 teaspoons turmeric
2 teaspoons cayenne pepper
1 tablespoon chili powder
1 teaspoon brown sugar
¼ cup Ginger and Red Pepper Sherry (page 39)
2 teaspoons soy sauce
1 pound large shrimp, peeled and deveined, tail segment left intact

Heat the oil in a wok or skillet over medium-high heat and add the garlic, ginger, and onion. Sauté until the onion is translucent, about 5 minutes. Add the remaining ingredients except the shrimp and cook over low heat, stirring, for 4 to 5 minutes. Allow the mixture to cool.

Add the shrimp, turn to coat evenly, cover, and refrigerate for several hours or overnight. Prepare a charcoal fire or preheat the gas grill. Thread four shrimp on each of four or five bamboo skewers. Grill over medium-hot coals about 4 to 6 minutes, turning once.

SERVES 4 TO 5

Japanese Grilled Beef

This appetizer relies on wasabi powder for much of its heat. Plan on marinating the beef a day ahead of time to allow the flavors to permeate the meat.

1 pound beef flank steak sliced across the grain into ⅛ inch thick strips
1 tablespoon finely minced garlic
1 teaspoon freshly grated ginger
2 teaspoons sugar
2 tablespoons wasabi powder (available in Asian groceries)
2 tablespoons soy sauce
⅓ cup Ginger Garlic Sherry (page 39)
1 teaspoon cornstarch
1 tablespoon cold water

Place the beef in a shallow baking dish. Combine the garlic, ginger, sugar, wasabi, soy sauce, and sherry and pour this over the beef. Cover, refrigerate, and allow to marinate overnight.

Thread the beef onto bamboo skewers that have been soaked for 45 minutes to prevent their burning. Reserve the marinade. Prepare a charcoal fire or preheat the gas grill.

While the fire is getting ready, mix the cornstarch with the water. Heat the reserved marinade in a saucepan over medium-high heat and add the cornstarch mixture. Heat,

stirring, over medium heat until the sauce thickens. Set aside and keep warm.

Grill the beef over medium-hot coals until it is slightly charred on the outside. Serve with the sauce.

SERVES 4 TO 6

Thai-style Meatballs in Red Curry

This is a nifty appetizer that's relatively quick and easy and definitely delicious.

½ pound lean ground beef
½ pound lean ground pork
1 teaspoon cayenne pepper
1 teaspoon ground coriander
1 teaspoon freshly ground black pepper
1 teaspoon finely minced garlic
2 teaspoons finely minced fresh basil
2 teaspoons finely minced fresh mint
2 tablespoons Curry Oil (page 20)
2 tablespoons Thai red curry paste (available in Asian groceries)
2 tablespoons peanut butter
2 teaspoons sugar
1 teaspoon tamarind paste (available in Asian groceries)
1 cup coconut milk
2 teaspoons fish sauce (available in Asian groceries)

In a mixing bowl combine the beef, pork, cayenne, coriander, pepper, garlic, 1 teaspoon of the basil and 1 teaspoon of the mint. Mix well and form the meat into 20 to 24 meatballs.

Heat the oil in a wok or skillet over medium-high heat and fry the meatballs until they are browned on the outside and cooked through, about 8 to 10 minutes. Remove them from the skillet. Drain off all but 1 tablespoon of the fat. Add the curry paste, peanut butter, sugar, tamarind paste, coconut milk, and fish sauce. Cook, stirring, over medium heat, 5 to 6 minutes. Add the remaining 1 teaspoon of basil and mint. Return the meatballs to the skillet and warm through, about 2 to 3 minutes. Serve in the sauce.

SERVES 6 TO 8

CHAPTER FIVE

Pork, Beef, and Lamb Entrées

Carolina Pulled Pork Barbecue

Battles have been fought over the proper way to barbecue pork. This recipe is a North Carolina tradition. The name "pulled pork" refers to the fact that the pork is cooked *very* slowly and thus is so tender that it can literally be pulled from the bone with a fork.

1 tablespoon salt
1 tablespoon sugar
1 tablespoon brown sugar
1 tablespoon freshly ground black pepper
1 tablespoon cayenne pepper
1 tablespoon paprika
1 teaspoon ground cumin
1 teaspoon onion powder
1 teaspoon garlic powder
One 4- to 5-pound boneless pork butt
1 cup North Carolina-style Cayenne Vinegar
   (page 31)

Mix well all the ingredients except the pork and vinegar and rub into the pork butt. Prepare a slow charcoal fire or stoke up the gas grill. The idea here is to cook the meat very slowly. The fire should never kiss the meat.

On a charcoal grill build the fire to one side or on a gas grill light the burner on the opposite side from where you place the meat. In either case throw a few hickory chips on the fire now and then to give it that marvelous sweet smoke that means barbecue. Cover the grill and cook until the meat registers 165°F to 170°F and is fork-tender, 5 to 7 hours. A charcoal fire will need refueling now and then but a gas fire need only be set to its lowest setting and you can basically forget it until it's time to check the meat.

When the meat is done, chop or shred it and mix with the vinegar, pile high on bread, buns, or rolls, and serve with hot pepper sauce on the side.

SERVES 8 TO 10

Pork Tenderloin with Green Curry

You might have to visit your local Asian grocer for some of the ingredients in this recipe but the search will be well worth it. If you cannot find the lime leaves and lemon grass try substituting the zest of a lemon and lime.

¼ *cup green curry paste (recipe follows)*
½ *cup Rice Wine Vinegar with Ginger (page 33)*
2 tablespoons lime juice
2 to 3 teaspoons finely chopped hot green chili peppers or to taste
1 stalk lemon grass, bottom third only, finely chopped
8 to 10 fresh mint leaves, shredded
Four 8-ounce pieces pork tenderloin

Mix together the curry paste, vinegar, lime juice, peppers, lemon grass, and mint. Butterfly the pieces of pork tenderloin by cutting them down the center lengthwise, to within ½ inch of the other side. Place the pieces of pork in a plastic bag one at a time and flatten them with a meat mallet until they are about ½ inch thick. When properly cut and flattened each piece should be an almost perfect rectangle of even thickness.

Place the pieces of meat in a baking dish and pour the marinade over them. Turn to coat. Cover and refrigerate. You can prepare the recipe up this point as much as a day ahead, or you can get your grill ready and start cooking as soon as the fire is right. The longer the meat marinates the more flavorful it becomes, but the marinade is so pungent that even a half hour is enough to give the pork a wonderful and exotic flavor. Grill the pork over medium coals until no longer pink inside, about 6 to 8 minutes.

SERVES 4

Green Curry Paste

¼ *cup chopped green chilies*
¼ *cup minced shallots*
2 tablespoons minced garlic
1 tablespoon shredded fresh ginger
¼ *cup chopped cilantro (fresh coriander), with roots*
4 to 5 kaffir lime leaves, shredded
3 tablespoons shredded lemon grass
1 tablespoon freshly ground black pepper
1 teaspoon ground coriander
½ *teaspoon ground cumin*
1 tablespoon fish sauce (available in Asian groceries)
¼ *cup vegetable oil (any bland variety such as sunflower, safflower, or soy)*

Process all the ingredients except the fish sauce and oil in a food processor until a coarse paste forms. With the machine running, add the fish sauce and oil in a stream and process until just blended. The mixture keeps well for several days if covered and refrigerated.

MAKES ABOUT 1 CUP

Grilled Pork Loin Chops with Tequila Lime Sauce

This recipe can be grilled outdoors or prepared in the broiler. Although the margarita-style overtones bring to mind balmy southwestern breezes, just the aroma of this dish in the broiler can bring a little sunny warmth to a blustery winter's day.

4 boneless center-cut pork loin chops, cut 1½ inches thick

2 tablespoons Fines Herbes Vinegar (page 27)

¼ cup fresh lime juice

¼ cup tequila

2 tablespoons minced shallots

2 teaspoons minced garlic

1 teaspoon dried rosemary, crushed

1 fresh jalapeño pepper, cored, seeded, and finely minced

2 tablespoons Green Herb Oil (page 21)

Salt and freshly ground black pepper to taste

Place the pork chops in a baking dish and add the remaining ingredients. Marinate several hours or overnight. Grill the chops over medium-hot coals until they are just barely pink in the center, about 10 minutes.

While the chops are grilling, pour the marinade into a large skillet and cook over medium-high heat until it is reduced by half. Pour 2 to 3 tablespoons of the sauce on each of four serving plates and place a grilled chop on each and serve immediately.

SERVES 4

Baby Back Ribs

True baby back ribs come from the loin of the pig. They are not simply small spareribs, but rather the rib bones behind the center part of the loin. An easy way to tell if what you are buying are really baby backs is to check the bone size and shape. Baby-back rib bones are more or less round, whereas spareribs tend to be flatter. Baby backs owe their cachet to the fact that they are leaner and tastier than their larger cousins.

1 cup Rice Wine Vinegar with Garlic (page 33)

½ cup frozen orange juice concentrate, thawed

½ cup Ginger and Red Pepper Sherry (page 39)

2 tablespoons minced garlic

2 tablespoons freshly grated ginger

1 tablespoon crushed dried red pepper

2 serrano peppers, minced

1 tablespoon coarsely ground black pepper

2 tablespoons soy sauce

2 tablespoons Sesame Oil with Szechwan Peppercorns (page 23)

5 pounds baby back ribs

1 tablespoon cornstarch

In a mixing bowl, combine the vinegar, orange juice concentrate, sherry, garlic, ginger, red pepper, serranos, black pepper, soy sauce, and oil. Place the ribs in a baking dish large enough to hold them in one layer. Pour the marinade ingredients over the ribs, cover, and marinate, refrigerated, overnight.

Prepare a charcoal fire or preheat a gas grill. Drain the ribs and place over medium-hot coals. Reserve the marinade. Grill, turning once or twice, until the ribs are cooked through, about 15 minutes. While the ribs are grilling, pour 1 cup of the marinade into a saucepan and add the cornstarch. Cook, stirring, over medium heat until the sauce thickens. When the ribs are almost done, baste with the sauce. Put the ribs on a serving platter, baste with the remaining sauce, and serve.

SERVES 5 TO 6

Pork Piccata

Piccata is a classic way of preparing veal. The same technique can be used for a vari-

ety of meat or poultry. Pork loin takes well to this preparation because it is lean and mild.

1 pound pork loin
2 tablespoons all-purpose flour
1 teaspoon freshly ground black pepper
1 teaspoon salt
2 tablespoons Lemon Thyme Oil (page 22)
¼ cup Allspice-flavored Sherry (page 37)
2 tablespoons lemon juice
2 tablespoons minced fresh parsley

Cut the pork loin into ½-inch-thick slices. Flatten the slices with a meat mallet to ⅛ inch thick. Combine the flour, pepper, and salt. Dust the pork slices in the flour and shake off the excess.

Heat the oil in a skillet over medium heat. Sauté the pork slices, turning once, until cooked through, 5 to 6 minutes. Remove the pork to a serving platter and keep warm. Add the sherry and lemon juice to the skillet and reduce over high heat by one third. Pour the sauce over the pork, garnish with parsley, and serve.

SERVES 4

Pork Cutlets with Spicy Plum Sauce

Pork cutlets cut from the loin or sirloin are lean, tender, and flavorful. Sirloin chops, especially, have a flavor of their own which is distinctive enough to stand up to the assertiveness of the plum sauce. Be forewarned: this sauce is spicy!

1 tablespoon Ginger Spice Oil (page 21)
2 tablespoons minced garlic

Grilled Pork Chops with Mango

2 tablespoons freshly grated ginger
¼ cup shallots, finely chopped
4 or 5 Thai bird peppers (or similar very hot fresh chilies), finely chopped, including seeds
One 16-ounce can pitted purple plums, finely chopped
¼ cup soy sauce
¼ cup Ground Hot Pepper Vinegar (page 29)
2 tablespoons chopped cilantro (fresh coriander)
4 boneless pork cutlets, about 8 ounces each

In a saucepan, heat the oil over medium heat and add the garlic, ginger, shallots, and bird peppers. Sauté for 2 to 3 minutes. Add the plums, soy sauce, and vinegar. Bring to a boil, reduce the heat, and simmer gently until the sauce is reduced and coats the back of a spoon. Remove from the heat and stir in the cilantro.

Prepare a fire and grill the cutlets until they are just barely pink in the center, about 12 to 15 minutes. Spoon half the sauce onto a serving platter and place the cutlets on top of the sauce. Pass the remaining sauce at the table.

SERVES 4

Grilled Pork Chops with Mango

Mangoes have been used in chutneys in India for centuries. Their slightly tart sweetness provides a wonderful counterpoint to the vinegar and spices traditionally used in chutneys.

4 bone-in center-cut pork chops, about 1 inch thick

1 tablespoon Sesame Oil with Szechwan Peppercorns *(page 23)*

Salt and freshly ground black pepper to taste

2 large, ripe mangoes, peeled, pitted, and coarsely chopped

1 small red onion, peeled and coarsely chopped

2 cloves garlic, finely chopped

2 serrano peppers, seeded and finely chopped

2 tablespoons Ginger and Red Pepper Sherry (page 39)

2 tablespoons Ginger Garlic Vinegar (page 29)

1 tablespoon coarsely ground black pepper

¼ cup chopped cilantro (fresh coriander)

Rub the chops with the oil and sprinkle with salt and pepper. In a mixing bowl, combine the remaining ingredients.

Prepare a fire and grill the chops, turning once, until they are just barely pink in the center, about 15 to 20 minutes. Spoon 1 tablespoon of the mango chutney on each of four serving dishes and place a chop next to it. Pass the remaining chutney at the table.

S E R V E S 4

Pork Kabobs with Chili Plum Sauce

Boneless pork sirloin chops are the best cut of meat to use for this recipe because they have just enough fat to stay tender after grilling. Boneless pork loin sometimes dries out during grilling.

1 pound boneless pork sirloin chops, cut into 1-inch pieces

⅔ cup plum preserves

¼ cup Rice Wine Vinegar with Garlic (page 33)

2 teaspoons finely minced garlic

2 teaspoons crushed dried red pepper or to taste

1 tablespoon soy sauce

2 tablespoons Sesame Oil with Szechwan Peppercorns (page 23)

2 tablespoons toasted sesame seeds

Soak 4 bamboo skewers in water for 30 minutes to 1 hour. Thread an equal amount of pork on each skewer. Combine all remaining ingredients except the sesame seeds.

Prepare a charcoal fire or preheat a gas grill. When the fire is ready, cook the pork over medium heat, basting with the sauce frequently, until the pork is cooked through, about 10 to 12 minutes. Sprinkle the toasted sesame seeds over the pork and serve.

S E R V E S 4

Pork Kabobs with Mango Pineapple Chili Sauce

Mangos have a slight tenderizing effect on meat. This recipe has a decidedly South Seas flavor that begs for a warm summer's eve, something ice cold with rum in it, and, if you can manage it, some waves lapping against the soft white sand of a beach far from anywhere. Well, you might have to imagine the beach and sea foam, but you can definitely enjoy this dish regardless.

1 pound boneless pork sirloin chops, cut into 1-inch cubes

1 mango, peeled and flesh scraped from the pit

1 cup pineapple juice
¼ cup freshly squeezed lime juice
¼ cup Ginger Garlic Sherry (page 39)
2 cloves garlic, minced
1 teaspoon minced fresh ginger
1 tablespoon soy sauce
1 tablespoon brown sugar
4 to 5 fresh red chili peppers, such as serrano
¼ cup Ginger Spice Oil (page 21)
¼ cup minced cilantro (fresh coriander)

Place the pork cubes in a shallow baking dish. In a food processor or blender, combine the mango flesh, pineapple juice, lime juice, sherry, garlic, ginger, soy sauce, brown sugar, and chili peppers. Process until smooth. Slowly add the oil in a thin stream with the processor running until the marinade is thoroughly blended.

Add the cilantro (do not process) and pour about two thirds of the marinade over the meat. Stir the cubes to coat them well, cover, and refrigerate several hours or overnight. Reserve the remaining marinade for basting while the meat is cooking.

Prepare a charcoal fire or preheat a gas grill. Thread the pork on metal or bamboo skewers. (If using bamboo skewers be sure to soak them in water for about 1 hour before using.) Cook the kabobs over medium-hot coals, basting and turning often, until they are lightly charred on the outside and cooked through, about 8 to 10 minutes.

SERVES 4

Fresh Ham with Hunter's Sauce

Fresh ham is often available at a bargain price because many people don't quite know what to do with it. One neat thing about fresh ham is that with the right ingredients you can almost make it taste like wild boar, a delicacy that few people ever have the opportunity to sample. This recipe makes a lot simply because the cut of meat is large.

One 8- to 9-pound fresh ham, trimmed
2 cups Provençal Vinegar (page 31)
1 cup Allspice-flavored Sherry (page 37)
1 tablespoon juniper berries
2 bay leaves
1 tablespoon whole black peppercorns
Sprig fresh thyme
1 small onion, peeled and coarsely chopped
4 cloves garlic, peeled and crushed
1 teaspoon salt

Place the ham in a large oven roasting bag. Add the remaining ingredients, tie the bag, and refrigerate overnight.

Preheat the oven to 325°F. Drain the ham and reserve the marinade. Place the ham on a rack in a large baking pan. Bake, uncovered, until a meat thermometer registers 170°F, about 30 minutes per pound. When the ham is done remove it from the oven and allow it to rest at room temperature for 15 minutes before carving.

While the ham is resting, strain the reserved marinade through a sieve into a saucepan. Cook the marinade over medium-high heat until it is reduced by half. Pass this sauce at the table with the carved ham.

SERVES 10 TO 12

Cajun-style Smoked Sausage with Hot-and-Sour Vegetables

If you're lucky enough to be able to find some Cajun smoked (andouille) sausage at your local meat market, great. Most people, however, might have to substitute smoked kielbasa (Polish sausage). This recipe will definitely work with the latter, but the real McCoy is worth searching out.

2 tablespoons peanut oil
1 pound Cajun smoked sausage (andouille), cut into 1-inch pieces
1 red bell pepper, cored, seeded, and cut into ½-inch chunks
1 green bell pepper, cored, seeded, and cut into ½-inch chunks
1 large white onion, peeled and cut into chunks
½ cup Rice Wine Vinegar with Garlic (page 33)
1 cup pineapple juice
½ cup ketchup
1 teaspoon crushed dried red pepper
1 teaspoon freshly ground black pepper
1 teaspoon ground cumin
¼ cup chicken stock
2 tablespoons cornstarch
¼ cup minced cilantro (fresh coriander)

Heat a wok or skillet over medium-high heat and add the oil. When the oil is almost smoking add the sausage and cook until slightly brown, about 2 to 3 minutes. Add the red and green peppers and the onion. Stir-fry for 2 minutes over medium-high heat.

Mix together the the remaining ingredients, except the cilantro, and add to the wok. Cook, stirring, over medium-high heat, until the sauce begins to thicken, about 2 minutes. Add the cilantro, stir through, and serve.

Serves 4

Ziti with Dandelion Greens and Italian Sausage

Dandelion greens are a blessing or a curse depending upon whether you look at them gastronomically or horticulturally. The simple solution to getting rid of them in your lawn, of course, is just pluck 'em and eat 'em.

1 pound fresh hot or sweet Italian sausage
1 large bunch fresh dandelion greens, about 8 to 10 cups, very coarsely chopped
1 tablespoon Garlic Basil Vinegar (page 29)
1 tablespoon Fennel Oil (page 20)
¼ cup tomato paste
Salt and freshly ground black pepper to taste
1 pound ziti cooked al dente
1 cup freshly grated Parmesan cheese

Remove the sausage from its casing and brown it in a Dutch oven over medium-high heat. Pour off all but 1 tablespoon of accumulated fat. Wash the dandelion greens and add them to the pot with the water that clings to them. Cover and cook over low heat until the greens are wilted.

Mix the vinegar, oil, and tomato paste to the greens and heat through. Add the cooked ziti to the pot and cook over low heat, stirring, until the pasta is heated through. Add half the cheese to the pasta and toss. Serve with the remaining cheese passed at the table.

Serves 6

Rolled Boneless Breast of Veal with Mushroom Stuffing

Many people have sworn off veal because of the inhumane conditions under which many of the veal calves are raised. Search out naturally raised, free-range veal. The meat is not as white as some commercial veal, but it is tender and sweet and you have the satisfaction of knowing that it was raised humanely.

If you've never boned a veal breast before, have your butcher do it for you. (Tell him you want the bones—they make excellent stock.)

One 4- to 5-pound whole veal breast, boned
Salt and freshly ground black pepper to taste
2 tablespoons Allspice and Bay Oil (page 17)
1 small onion, peeled and coarsely chopped
2 cloves garlic, coarsely chopped
8 ounces fresh mushrooms, coarsely chopped
Salt and freshly ground white pepper to taste
¼ cup minced fresh parsley

Spread the veal out on a flat surface, boned side facing up, and sprinkle it with salt and pepper to taste. Heat 1 tablespoon of the oil in a skillet over medium heat and sauté the onion, garlic, and mushrooms until the mushrooms have given up their liquid and it evaporates, about 5 to 6 minutes. Add salt and pepper to taste. Add the parsley.

Spread the mushroom mixture over the flattened veal breast. Roll up the breast, jelly-roll fashion and tie it at 2-inch intervals with butcher twine. Coat the outside of the breast with the remaining oil. Sprinkle the outside with white pepper and salt to taste.

Place the breast in a roasting pan and roast, uncovered, at 350°F until a meat thermometer registers 160°F, approximately 1½ to 2 hours. Allow the roast to sit for 10 minutes before carving.

SERVES 6

Veal Oreganata

Veal oreganata is a classic Italian dish that combines sweet veal, pungent oregano, and chunky ripe tomatoes. Feel free to substitute chicken for the veal, if you so desire.

1 tablespoon Pizza Oil (page 22)
4 cups tomato puree
Six ¼-inch-thick veal cutlets, about 8 ounces each
6 medium-size potatoes, unpeeled, cut into 1-inch chunks
1 green bell pepper, cored, seeded, and diced
1 red bell pepper, cored, seeded, and diced
1 small onion, peeled and coarsely chopped
4 cloves garlic, peeled and coarsely chopped
1 cup Lemon Mint Sherry (page 41)
1 tablespoon dried oregano
1 tablespoon minced fresh parsley
Salt and freshly ground black pepper to taste

Preheat the oven to 375°F.

Spread the oil evenly across the bottom of a baking pan. Pour 1 cup of the tomato puree evenly across the bottom of the pan. Place the veal cutlets in a single layer over the tomato puree. Add all the remaining ingredients, distributing them evenly over the veal cutlets. Pour the remaining tomato sauce over all.

Bake, uncovered, until the meat and

potatoes are tender, about 1 hour. Serve the meat, potatoes, and peppers together on a serving platter and pass the sauce separately at the table.

S E R V E S   6

Lemon Veal

This is another veal dish in which boneless, skinless chicken breasts would be an all-right substitute.

6 veal cutlets, cut ¼ inch thick, about 8 ounces each
¼ cup Lemon Mint Sherry (page 41)
Flour for dusting
2 tablespoons Lemon Thyme Oil (page 22)
2 cloves garlic, finely minced
1 teaspoon grated lemon zest
1 teaspoon thyme leaves
Salt and freshly ground black pepper to taste

Marinate the veal cutlets in the sherry for several hours or overnight, covered, in the refrigerator. Drain the veal, reserving the marinade. Dust the cutlets with flour, shaking off the excess.

Heat the oil in a skillet over medium heat. Add the garlic, lemon zest, and thyme leaves. Add the veal cutlets and sauté over medium heat until the veal is cooked through, about 5 to 7 minutes, turning midway through cooking. Remove the veal to a serving platter and cover lightly with foil to keep warm. Increase the heat to high and add the reserved marinade. Cook, stirring, until the liquid is reduced by about two

thirds. Pour the liquid over the veal, season with salt and pepper, and serve immediately.

S E R V E S   4

Stir-fried Beef and Snow Peas with Bird Pepper Sherry

A staple of Chinese cooking, snow peas are sweet, tender, almost translucent, young peas, that can be eaten raw in salads as well.

¼ cup Rice Wine Vinegar with Garlic (page 33)
1 tablespoon sugar
¼ cup soy sauce
One 2-inch piece fresh ginger, peeled and coarsely chopped
1 pound beef flank steak, cut thinly across the grain
¼ cup Bird Pepper Sherry (page 38)
1 tablespoon cornstarch
2 tablespoons peanut oil
1 cup snow peas
1 red bell pepper, cored, seeded, and cut into ½-inch wide strips
4 scallions, cut into 1-inch pieces

Combine the vinegar, sugar, soy sauce, and ginger in a bowl. Put the beef in another bowl, combine the sherry and cornstarch and pour it over the beef. Marinate for at least ½ hour, covered, at room temperature.

Heat the peanut oil in a wok over medium-high heat. When almost smoking, drain the beef and add it to the wok. Reserve the marinade. Stir-fry until the beef begins

Stir-fried Beef and Snow Peas with Bird Pepper Sherry

to brown, 2 to 3 minutes. Add the snow peas, pepper, and scallions. Stir-fry for 1 to 2 minutes. Add the reserved marinade and the vinegar mixture. Stir-fry until the sauce thickens slightly, 2 to 3 minutes. Serve immediately.

SERVES 4

Beef Ribs with Sherry and Caraway

One doesn't usually associate the flavor of caraway with beef but this combination seems to work splendidly. Ask your butcher for the long ribs from a standing rib roast instead of using what are commonly referred to as "short ribs." The ribs from the back of a standing roast have more flavor because all the meat is close to the bone.

8 beef ribs
¾ cup Allspice-flavored Sherry (page 37)
2 tablespoons Allspice and Bay Oil (page 17)
1 tablespoon caraway seed
Salt and freshly ground black pepper to taste

Place the ribs in deep bowl or baking dish. Add the sherry, oil, caraway seeds, salt, and pepper. Cover and marinate overnight in the refrigerator.

Preheat the oven to 375°F. Drain the ribs and reserve the marinade. Place the ribs in a baking pan and roast, uncovered, until they are browned and crispy on the outside and just cooked through, 30 to 40 minutes. While the ribs are roasting, cook the reserved marinade in a saucepan over medium-high heat until the liquid is reduced by half.

When the ribs are done, pour this sauce over them and serve.

SERVES 4

Fiery Fajitas

The fajita craze that thrust itself on the food world in the mid-eighties shows no sign of abating. It started in the Southwest—Texas, to be exact—and from there spread all over the country. To be perfectly authentic you should use beef skirt steak. Flank steak makes an appropriate substitute since the texture is similar, although the flavor is a little different. The secret to ravenously delicious fajitas is allowing the meat to marinate at least several hours, or, preferably, overnight.

1 pound skirt or flank steak
3 tablespoons Sesame Oil with Szechwan Peppercorns (page 23)
2 tablespoons lime juice
3 tablespoons chopped cilantro (fresh coriander)
1 teaspoon cayenne pepper
3 cloves garlic, finely minced
Eight 10-inch flour tortillas
2 large red onions, cut in half vertically and cut into strips
1 red bell pepper, cored, seeded, and sliced into julienne strips
1 green bell pepper, cored, seeded, and sliced into julienne strips
¼ cup fresh or pickled jalapeño pepper slices
½ cup salsa
½ cup guacamole

Place the steak in a baking dish and add 1 tablespoon of the oil, the lime juice, cilantro, cayenne pepper, and garlic. Turn the meat to coat evenly with the marinade. Cover and refrigerate several hours or overnight.

When you are ready to assemble the fajitas, wrap the tortillas in a damp (not wet) dish towel and place in a microwave oven on warm for 5 to 6 minutes, or simply place them on a baking sheet in a preheated oven at 250°F for the same length of time.

Preheat a cast-iron skillet over high heat until it is very hot. Add 1 tablespoon of oil. Drain the steak from the marinade and reserve the marinade. When the oil is almost smoking, add the steak and cook 2 to 3 minutes on one side and then turn. Cook 2 to 3 minutes on the other side for medium-rare. Place the steak on a carving board and cover with foil to keep warm.

Add the remaining 1 tablespoon of oil to the skillet. Sauté the onions and peppers quickly over high heat to char slightly. Do not overcook. Add the reserved marinade and cook 1 to 2 minutes longer. Remove the vegetables to a serving platter.

Slice the steak across the grain into thin strips. To serve, put some beef in the center of a tortilla. Add some onions and peppers, salsa and guacamole. Fold one end up about halfway and then fold the sides over to the center.

SERVES 4

Szechwan-style Roast Beef Tenderloin

This is a twist on that classic French dish, usually prepared for two, Châteaubriand.

The term *Châteaubriand* actually refers to a method of cooking a piece of beef, but has commonly come to refer to the piece of meat itself. This cut of beef is the large, or butt, end of a beef tenderloin. This recipe uses pungent Szechwan-style spices to add verve and zing (not to mention heat) to what is probably one of the blandest cuts of beef on the steer.

1 beef tenderloin roast, about 1½ to 2 pounds
2 tablespoons Sesame Oil with Szechwan Peppercorns (page 23)
¼ cup Ground Hot Pepper Vinegar (page 29)
1 tablespoon whole black peppercorns
1 tablespoon whole white peppercorns
1 serrano pepper, chopped
1 tablespoon soy sauce
1 tablespoon chopped garlic

Place the roast in a large, sturdy plastic bag (an oven browning bag is ideal for this). Add the remaining ingredients. Close the bag, refrigerate, and allow to marinate overnight.

Prepare a charcoal fire or preheat a gas grill. Grill the roast approximately 20 minutes per pound for medium-rare, or until a meat thermometer registers 140°F. Let the roast rest for 5 to 10 minutes before carving.

SERVES 4 TO 6

Hunan-style Meatballs

These spicy beef balls are a staple of Hunan Chinese cooking. They make a great addition to a multicourse Chinese meal or they can serve as an appetizer.

For the meatballs:

1 pound lean ground beef
1 small onion, peeled and finely chopped
2 cloves garlic, finely minced
1 egg
½ cup plain dry bread crumbs
¼ cup Ginger and Red Pepper Sherry (page 39)
½ teaspoon salt
1 teaspoon freshly ground black pepper
¼ cup peanut oil

For the Hunan sauce:

1 teaspoon finely minced garlic
1 teaspoon freshly grated ginger
2 scallions, white part only, finely minced
2 tablespoons chili paste with garlic (available in Asian groceries)
2 teaspoons soy sauce
2 teaspoons Sesame Oil with Szechwan Peppercorns (page 23)
2 tablespoons Rice Wine Vinegar with Garlic (page 33)
3 tablespoons cornstarch
1 cup Ginger and Red Pepper Sherry (page 39)

In a mixing bowl combine all the meatball ingredients except the peanut oil and mix well. Form the meat mixture into 20 to 24 meatballs, about 1 inch in diameter. Heat the peanut oil in a skillet or wok over medium heat and fry the meatballs until they are golden brown. Pour off all but 1 tablespoon of fat from the skillet.

In the same skillet, add the garlic, ginger, and scallions and stir-fry over medium heat until the garlic just starts to brown. Add the chili paste, soy sauce, oil, and vinegar.

Cook, stirring, over medium heat for 2 to 3 minutes.

Mix the cornstarch with the sherry and pour it into the skillet. Cook, stirring, until the sauce thickens. Return the meatballs to the skillet and simmer them in the sauce until they are heated through, 3 to 4 minutes.

Serves 4 to 6

Steak Diane

Steak Diane is a classic preparation for beef. Traditionally, boneless rib-eye steaks are the cut of choice, but fillets work just as well. By the way, this recipe is not exactly low in fat or cholesterol, so either throw caution to the wind or save it for a special treat.

4 rib-eye steaks, cut ¾ inch thick, about 8 ounces each
Coarsely ground black pepper to coat
Salt
4 tablespoons (½ stick) butter
1 tablespoon Dijon-style mustard
¼ cup chopped shallots
2 tablespoons Worcestershire sauce
¼ cup Ginger Garlic Sherry (page 39)
2 tablespoons minced fresh chives

Coat the steaks with the black pepper, pressing it into the meat to make as much adhere as possible. Sprinkle with salt to taste.

Preheat a large cast-iron skillet over high heat until it starts smoking. Cook the steaks, turning once, about 3 minutes per side for medium-rare. When the steaks are done, place them on a serving platter and keep them warm.

Add the butter to the skillet and mix in the mustard as the butter melts. Add the remaining ingredients except the chives and cook, stirring, about 3 minutes. Pour the sauce over the steaks, garnish with the chives, and serve.

SERVES 4

Bulgogi (Korean-style Beef)

Bulgogi is a traditional staple in Korean homes. The preparation is fairly quick and straightforward. Use a good quality cut of beef such as top sirloin or flank steak.

1 pound boneless sirloin or flank steak, well trimmed
½ cup Rice Wine Vinegar with Garlic (page 33)
¼ cup soy sauce
1 teaspoon plus 2 tablespoons Sesame Oil with Szechwan Peppercorns (page 23)
¼ teaspoon freshly ground white pepper
1 teaspoon finely minced garlic
4 scallions, white part cut diagonally into 1-inch pieces and the green part finely minced
2 tablespoons toasted sesame seeds

Cut the beef across the grain into ⅛-inch-thick slices. Cut the slices into 2-inch pieces. Put the beef in a bowl and add the rice wine vinegar, soy sauce, 1 teaspoon of the oil, white pepper, and garlic. Marinate about 30 minutes to 1 hour.

Heat the 2 tablespoons of oil in a wok over high heat. Drain the beef, reserving the marinade, and stir-fry for 2 to 3 minutes. Add the white part of the onions and stir-fry

another minute. Add the reserved marinade and stir-fry 1 more minute. Sprinkle the minced green onion over the beef and serve.

SERVES 4

Mongolian Beef Barbecue

Mongolian cuisine tends to be as fiery as the hottest Thai food. Traditionally, Mongolian food is cooked over coals in outdoor braziers. Marinate the meat several hours or, better yet, overnight.

One 1- to 1½-pound flank steak
¼ cup Rice Wine Vinegar with Garlic (page 33)
2 teaspoons minced garlic
2 teaspoons freshly grated ginger
2 tablespoons soy sauce
2 tablespoons Sesame Oil with Szechwan Peppercorns (page 23)
2 to 3 fresh Thai bird peppers or other hot chilies

Put the flank steak in a baking dish. Combine the remaining ingredients and pour over the steak. Marinate at room temperature for several hours or refrigerate and marinate overnight. Turn the meat several times.

Prepare a charcoal fire or fire up the gas grill. Cook the steak over a very hot fire about 3 to 4 minutes on each side for medium rare, or cook to desired doneness. Carve the meat across the grain in thin slices and serve.

SERVES 4 TO 6

Thai Beef Curry

The word curry comes from the Tamil word *kari*, meaning "sauce." It is a catchall term that refers as much to a combination of ingredients as to a method of preparation. Although curries are indigenous to the Indian subcontinent, they have migrated into Far Eastern cookery, especially into Chinese and Thai cuisines.

1 whole red chili pepper (the hotter the better), finely chopped

1 teaspoon freshly ground black pepper

2 tablespoons chopped cilantro roots

1 scallion, finely minced

2 cloves garlic, finely minced

2 tablespoons minced lemon grass, bottom part only (available in Asian groceries)

4 to 5 Thai basil leaves, chopped (available in Asian groceries, but sweet basil can be substituted)

1 tablespoon Curry Oil (page 20)

1 pound flank steak, cut across the grain into ¼-inch slices

One 16-ounce can coconut cream

2 tablespoons fish sauce (available in Asian groceries)

2 tablespoons minced cilantro (fresh coriander)

With a mortar and pestle or in a food processor, grind together the chili pepper, black pepper, cilantro roots, scallion, garlic, lemon grass, basil, and curry oil.

In a wok, heat the coconut cream to boiling, reduce the heat to medium, and add the beef. Cook over medium heat for 15 to 20 minutes. Add the fish sauce and the curry mixture and cook another 5 minutes. Add the minced cilantro and serve.

SERVES 4

Braciole

Braciole (pronounced bra-chee-OH-le) is an Italian meat roll. It is traditionally made from beef flank steak and stuffed with herbs, spices, cheese, and sometimes hard-boiled eggs. Some Italians prefer to make their braciole from pork cutlets, and lately, from turkey breast slices. This recipe follows the more traditional route but feel free to experiment with different meats to suit your own tastes.

1 whole flank steak, about 1 to 1½ pounds

2 teaspoons finely minced garlic

2 teaspoons fresh basil leaves

2 teaspoons fresh oregano leaves

2 teaspoons fresh thyme leaves

1 teaspoon crushed fresh rosemary

1 teaspoon freshly ground black pepper

½ teaspoon salt

¼ cup freshly grated Parmesan cheese

¼ cup minced fresh parsley

2 tablespoons Pizza Oil (page 22)

1 small onion, finely chopped

One 28-ounce can Italian plum tomatoes packed in puree

1 teaspoon crushed dried red pepper

Lay the flank steak flat on a cutting board. With a thin-bladed, very sharp knife, begin cutting along one edge, working toward the center, essentially separating the steak into two layers. Do not cut all the way through the other end so that when the steak is spread out it is in one piece but double in size.

Sprinkle 1 teaspoon each of the garlic, basil, oregano, and thyme, the rosemary, black pepper, salt, Parmesan cheese, and parsley over the surface of the meat, leaving a 1-inch border all the way around.

Roll the meat up jelly-roll fashion, tucking in the ends as you go. Tie the meat in several places with butcher twine or secure with skewers. Heat the oil in a Dutch oven over medium heat. Brown the braciole on all sides, about 8 to 10 minutes. Add the onion and the remaining 1 teaspoon of garlic to the pot and sauté until just slightly brown, about 2 minutes.

Break up the plum tomatoes and add them along with their juice and the puree to the pot. Add the remaining teaspoons of basil, oregano, and thyme and the red pepper. Bring the sauce to a simmer and cook over low heat until the sauce is slightly thickened and the meat is tender, about 1 hour.

Slice the meat into ½-inch-thick slices, arrange it on a serving platter, and pour a little of the sauce over it. Pass the remaining sauce at the table or use it to dress some accompanying pasta.

SERVES 4 TO 6

Carpaccio with Garlic Basil Vinaigrette

Carpaccio is an Italian appetizer which classically consists of shavings of raw beef fillet drizzled with olive oil and lemon juice. If you have any missgivings about eating raw meat, you might as as well skip the rest of this recipe right now. The fact of the matter is that it's probably safe. I say probably because nothing is certain, but raw beef is only one tiny little step away from rare beef, so if you'd eat one you shouldn't have any problem with the other.

One little trick you can use to eliminate the possibility of any parasitic infection from raw meat is to do what some sushi chefs do with fish. If you put the meat in the freezer for a week or so at 0°F or below, this should kill any little beasties that might make you sick should they be present.

1 pound beef fillet
2 tablespoons Garlic Basil Vinegar (page 29)
1 teaspoon minced garlic
1 teaspoon Dijon-style mustard
2 teaspoons finely chopped shallots
⅓ cup Oil with Fines Herbes (page 21)
2 tablespoons capers, drained
¼ cup finely chopped sweet onion
¼ cup minced fresh basil
Freshly ground black pepper

Place the beef in the freezer (only if it hasn't already been frozen) for 45 minutes to 1 hour. This will partially freeze it to make it easier to slice thinly. Using a very sharp knife, slice the beef into ⅛-inch-thick slices. Place the slices between two sheets of plastic wrap and gently pound them with a meat mallet to make them about half as thick. Stack the slices between pieces of plastic wrap an refrigerate for at least 1 hour.

In a mixing bowl combine the vinegar, garlic, mustard, shallots, and oil. Whisk to blend.

Arrange an equal number of beef slices on four chilled plates. Divided the capers, onions, and basil among the four plates. Drizzle some vinaigrette over each, sprinkle with black pepper, and serve.

SERVES 4

Thai Beef Salad

This dish is a classic of Thai cooking. It makes a perfect first course as part of a dinner or as the main dish for lunch or a light supper. Traditionally it radiates quite a bit of heat due the inclusion of numerous Thai bird peppers, but if you substitute a milder chili you can tone down the heat considerably.

2 tablespoons lime juice
2 tablespoons Ground Hot Pepper Vinegar (page 29)
2 tablespoons finely chopped cilantro roots
½ teaspoon freshly ground black pepper
Four 4-ounce beef tenderloin steaks
8 cups shredded green leaf or romaine lettuce
1 small red onion, peeled, thinly sliced, and separated into rings
16 cherry tomatoes
¼ cup Rice Wine Vinegar with Lemon Grass and Kaffir Lime (page 33)
1 tablespoon fish sauce (available in Asian groceries)
3 to 4 Thai bird peppers, seeds included, minced (available in Asian groceries)
1 teaspoon crushed dried red pepper
⅓ cup Sesame Oil with Szechwan Peppercorns (page 23)
½ cup minced cilantro (fresh coriander)

Combine the lime juice, vinegar, cilantro roots, and pepper. Place the steaks in a shallow baking dish and pour the marinade ingredients over them. Turn to coat and marinate at room temperature for 1 hour.

Heat a heavy cast-iron skillet over high heat until it is smoking. Drain the steaks, pat dry and pan-grill them, turning once, until they are medium-rare, 4 to 6 minutes. Remove the steaks to a cutting board and when they have come to room temperature slice them into ⅛-inch-thick slices.

Divide the lettuce, onion, and tomatoes among four dinner plates. Arrange an equal amount of beef on each plate. In a bowl whisk together the remaining ingredients except the cilantro. Pour an equal amount of the dressing on each salad. Sprinkle the cilantro on each salad and serve. (The salads can be prepared ahead of time and refrigerated but don't add the dressing and cilantro until you are ready to serve them.)

SERVES 4

Marinated Leg of Lamb

Plan on doing the advance preparations for this dish a day or two ahead of time. The longer the lamb marinates, the more flavorful it becomes.

One 6- to 8-pound leg of lamb, boned and butterflied
1 cup Cinque Herbes Vinegar (page 27)
1 tablespoon freshly ground black pepper
4 to 5 cloves garlic, peeled and minced
¼ cup minced shallots
2 tablespoons fresh rosemary
¼ cup fresh mint leaves, shredded
¼ cup Green Herb Oil (page 21)

Place the leg of lamb in a casserole or, better yet, in a turkey-sized oven cooking bag. In a

Carpaccio with Garlic Basil Vinaigrette

bowl, mix the remaining ingredients. Pour over the lamb. Cover the casserole or tie the bag closed and refrigerate at least overnight, or up to 4 days.

Preheat the oven to 375°F. Remove the lamb from the marinade and pat dry. Reserve the marinade. Put the lamb on a roasting rack, fat side up, and roast for about 15 minutes per pound for medium-rare, or until it is the desired doneness when pierced with a knife in the thickest part of the flesh. Allow the lamb to rest 10 minutes before carving.

While the lamb is resting, strain the reserved marinade and cook it over high heat until it is reduced by half. Pass the sauce at the table with the carved lamb.

SERVES 8 TO 10

Roast Stuffed Leg of Lamb

A leg of lamb is a very versatile piece of meat. You can, of course, just rub it with some olive oil, sprinkle on a little salt and pepper, and pop it in the oven. But there's a whole range of other possibilities that can lift a leg of lamb from the ordinary to the sublime. Try this special recipe next time you need something special to serve.

1 whole, boneless, butterflied leg of lamb,
  about 4 to 6 pounds
4 tablespoons Provençal Oil (page 22)
1 small onion, peeled and finely chopped
2 teaspoons finely minced garlic
2 stalks celery, leaves included, finely chopped
¼ cup chopped pistachio nuts
¼ cup oil-packed sun-dried tomatoes, minced

Grated zest of 1 lemon
1 teaspoon dried thyme
1 teaspoon crushed rosemary
Salt and freshly ground black pepper to taste

Preheat the oven to 425°F. Spread the lamb out flat and trim away any fat on the inside. In a skillet heat 2 tablespoons of the oil over medium heat. Sauté the onion, garlic, and celery until the onion is translucent, about 3 to 4 minutes. Turn off the heat and stir in the nuts, tomatoes, and zest. Spread this mixture over the inside two thirds of the lamb surface. Roll up the lamb, tucking in the edges, and secure with butcher's twine in several places. Rub the outside surface of the lamb with the remaining 2 tablespoons of oil, and sprinkle with the thyme, rosemary, salt, and pepper.

Place the lamb on a roasting rack and roast for 15 minutes. Reduce the oven temperature to 350°F and roast approximately 1 to 1½ hours longer for medium to medium-rare doneness. Use a meat thermometer to be certain of the internal temperature. Allow the lamb to rest approximately 15 minutes before slicing.

SERVES 8 TO 10

Middle Eastern Lamb Patties

Mint, parsley, garlic, and cumin. These are the traditional flavorings paired with ground lamb in many classic Middle Eastern dishes. Serve it in pita bread with some cool yogurt and cucumber dressing and either harissa or your favorite hot sauce.

1 pound lean ground lamb
¼ cup chopped fresh mint leaves
¼ cup chopped fresh parsley
1 tablespoon minced garlic
½ teaspoon ground cumin
2 tablespoons Lemon Mint Sherry (page 41)
1 teaspoon freshly ground black pepper
Salt to taste
1 cup plain low-fat yogurt
½ cup chopped cucumber
4 pita breads
Hot sauce

In a mixing bowl combine the lamb, mint, parsley, garlic, cumin, and sherry. Mix together well and form into four patties. Grill over medium-hot coals or broil until medium-rare, about 8 to 10 minutes minutes.

Combine the yogurt and cucumber. Place a patty in each pita bread, add ¼ cup dressing, and serve with hot sauce.

SERVES 4

Lamb Keftas

Keftas are a Moroccan favorite. Basically they are meatballs highly seasoned with various herbs and spices, skewered and grilled over a charcoal fire. The best way to enjoy keftas are in pita bread with a cooling yogurt-cucumber dressing. You may substitute beef in this recipe and still be authentic, or ground chicken or turkey, which is lower in fat and cholesterol and is equally delicious.

FOR THE KEFTAS:

1 pound lean ground lamb
1 small onion, peeled and finely chopped
1 teaspoon minced garlic
1 teaspoon finely minced fresh ginger
1 teaspoon ground cardamom
1 teaspoon ground allspice
1 teaspoon ground cloves
1 teaspoon ground cinnamon
1 teaspoon ground nutmeg
2 teaspoons ground cumin
2 teaspoons finely minced cilantro (fresh coriander)
2 teaspoons finely minced fresh mint
2 teaspoons freshly ground black pepper
1 tablespoon cayenne pepper
¼ cup Ginger and Red Pepper Sherry (page 39)

FOR THE CUCUMBER DRESSING:

8 ounces plain low-fat yogurt
¼ cup finely diced cucumber
1 tablespoon finely minced fresh mint

In a mixing bowl combine all the kefta ingredients and mix well to distribute evenly. Shape the mixture into about twenty 1-inch meatballs.

Thread 5 meatballs onto each of 4 bamboo skewers, which have been soaked in water for at least 1 hour.

Prepare a charcoal fire or preheat a gas grill. Grill the meatballs over medium-hot coals until just barely pink in the center, about 8 to 10 minutes.

Combine all the dressing ingredients and mix well. To serve the keftas, remove the meatballs from the skewers and place them in the pocket of 4 pieces of pita bread. Pour some of the yogurt-cucumber dressing on each and serve.

S E R V E S   4

Indian-style Lamb Curry

Indian curries come in all sorts and varieties. Their heat quotient ranges from tame to infernally hot. This recipe probably falls somewhere in the middle.

4 lamb steaks, about 1 inch thick, cut from the leg
¼ cup Ginger Garlic Vinegar (page 29)
2 teaspoons minced garlic
2 teaspoons freshly grated ginger
1 tablespoon cayenne pepper
1 tablespoon Ginger Spice Oil (page 21)
½ cup Ginger Garlic Sherry (page 39)
¼ cup chili sauce with garlic (available in Asian groceries)

4 medium-size potatoes, cut into 1-inch chunks
1 cup (approximately) cauliflower florets
1 large onion, cut into chunks
2 ripe tomatoes, cored and quartered
2 tablespoons minced cilantro (fresh coriander)

Arrange the lamb steaks in a shallow baking pan. Combine the vinegar, garlic, ginger, and cayenne and pour the mixture over the meat. Turn to coat. Marinate several hours or, preferably, overnight.

Heat the oil in a large skillet over high heat. Drain the steaks and sear them until they are brown on both sides, about 3 to 4 minutes per side. Reduce heat to medium and add the sherry and chili sauce. Arrange the potato chunks around the lamb, cover, and cook about 15 minutes. Add the cauliflower, onion, and tomatoes. Cover and cook another 15 minutes. Sprinkle the cilantro over all and serve.

S E R V E S   4

Poultry Entrées

Duck Breast with Fruited Brandy

This is an elegant dish which you can be proud to serve to company. Although duck is traditionally thought to be high in fat, the breast meat is the leanest part of the bird and this recipe uses it to advantage.

2 whole boneless duck breasts, halved, skin left intact
Salt and freshly ground black pepper to taste
4 tablespoons clarified butter
¼ cup chopped shallots
1 teaspoon fresh thyme
1 ½ cups cherry brandy
3 tablespoons Raspberry Lemon Vinegar (page 33)
One 10-ounce package frozen sweet cherries, thawed (substitute canned cherries if frozen are unavailable)
2 tablespoons cornstarch mixed in ¼ cup cold water
¼ cup fresh parsley, minced

Season the duck breasts with salt and pepper and sauté them in a large skillet in the butter over moderately high heat until they are crisp and brown on the outside and slightly pink in the center. Remove them to a serving platter and keep warm.

Drain off all but 2 tablespoons of the fat and add the shallots and thyme leaves and sauté briefly, about 2 minutes. Deglaze the pan with ½ cup of the brandy, stirring constantly over moderately high heat, until the liquid is almost evaporated, about 2 minutes. Add the remaining brandy, the vinegar, and the cherries with their juice and sauté until the liquid is slightly reduced, about 5 minutes. Add the cornstarch and water mixture and cook, stirring, until the sauce is thickened, about 2 to 3 minutes. Pour the cherry brandy sauce over the duck breasts, sprinkle with parsley, and serve.

SERVES 4

Garlic Ginger Turkey Steaks

Because people are watching their fat and cholesterol intake these days, turkey has taken on a special place in many people's di-

ets. Turkey is an extremely versatile meat but it can be rather dry and bland if it is not handled properly. Because turkey has so little natural fat care must be taken not to overcook it.

This recipe adds a modicum of fat in the flavored oil but it also adds a lot of flavor to what would otherwise be a rather bland dish.

4 turkey breast cutlets, about 4 to 6 ounces each
½ cup Ginger Garlic Sherry (page 38)
1 teaspoon minced garlic
1 teaspoon freshly grated ginger
Salt and freshly ground black pepper to taste
2 tablespoons Provençal Oil (page 22)

Place the turkey steaks in a baking dish and add the sherry, garlic, ginger, salt, and pepper. Marinate, covered, for at least 1 hour, or overnight in the refrigerator.

Drain the turkey cutlets and reserve the marinade. Heat the oil in a skillet and sauté the cutlets over medium-high heat until they are almost cooked through, 5 to 7 minutes. Add the reserved marinade and simmer until the liquid is reduced slightly, another 5 to 6 minutes. Serve the cutlets with the pan juices.

SERVES 4

Honey Gingered Chicken

This dish has classic Szechwan overtones. The hot chili oil gives it a pleasant bite and the honey-ginger sauce tempers the spiciness. Make the sauce first and set it aside while preparing the chicken.

Duck Breast with Fruited Brandy

FOR THE SAUCE (MAKES ABOUT 2½ CUPS):

1 tablespoon Chili Oil with Garlic (page 19)
1 teaspoon freshly grated ginger
½ cup ketchup
4 tablespoons honey
1 tablespoon soy sauce
2 tablespoons dry sherry
2 tablespoons rice wine vinegar
3 tablespoons cornstarch
1 cup chicken broth

FOR THE CHICKEN:

1 cup all-purpose flour
1 teaspoon celery salt
1 teaspoon freshly ground white pepper
4 boneless, skinless chicken breast halves, about 1½ pounds total, each cut into 4 pieces
2 tablespoons Chili Oil with Garlic (page 19)
2 tablespoons peanut oil
1 teaspoon finely minced fresh ginger
2 teaspoons finely minced garlic
1 large white onion, cut into large dice, about 1½ cups
1 cup diagonally cut ¼-inch peeled carrot slices
1 cup diagonally cut ½-inch celery slices
1 large red or green bell pepper, cored, seeded, and cut into ½-inch pieces, about 1 cup
2 tablespoons soy sauce
2 tablespoons dry sherry

To make the sauce, heat the oil in a wok over medium-high heat and add the ginger. Stir-fry 1 minute and add the remaining ingredients except the chicken broth and cornstarch. Stir-fry 1 to 2 minutes. Mix the cornstarch and chicken broth and add it to the wok. Cook, stirring, until the sauce thickens. Pour the sauce into a serving bowl and wipe the wok clean before proceeding.

To prepare the chicken, mix the flour with the celery salt and pepper in a plastic bag. Add the chicken pieces, a few at a time, and shake until coated evenly. Shake off the excess flour. Heat the oils in a wok over medium-high heat and when it is hot stir-fry the chicken pieces, a few at a time, until they are golden and crisp on the outside and cooked through, about 2 to 3 minutes. Remove the pieces with a slotted spoon and keep warm.

Add the ginger, garlic, and onion to the wok and stir-fry 1 minute. Add the carrot, celery, and pepper and stir-fry until the vegetables are crisp-tender, 2 minutes. Add the soy sauce and sherry and stir-fry 1 minute. Add the reserved chicken and stir-fry 1 minute.

Spoon half the honey-ginger sauce over the chicken and vegetables, stirring to coat evenly, and transfer the mixture to a serving bowl. Pass the remaining sauce at the table.

S E R V E S 4

Roast Garlic Lemon Chicken

It seems that lately most chicken recipes call for boneless, skinless breast meat. Certainly for the absolute minimum amount of fat and for the simplest and quickest cooking times, boneless breasts can't be beat. But there is something to be said for chicken on the bone. For one thing, it has more flavor. For another thing, bone-in chicken is juicier.

One 5- to 7-pound roasting chicken
1 lemon
4 cloves garlic
Salt to taste
¼ cup Rice Wine Vinegar with Garlic (page 33)
¼ cup Allspice-flavored Sherry (page 37)

Preheat the oven to 350°F. Wash the chicken under cold running water and dry thoroughly. Cut the lemon in half and rub the halves all over the chicken. Peel and slightly crush the garlic cloves. Rub one or two of them all over the chicken.

Put the lemon halves and garlic in the chicken cavity and truss the chicken by bending the wings underneath and bringing the legs together and tying them securely. Place the chicken on a roasting rack and roast, uncovered, for about 20 minutes per pound, or until a meat thermometer registers 180°F.

When the chicken is done, tip it to allow the juices in the cavity to flow into the roasting pan. Put the chicken aside to rest for 15 minutes before carving. Degrease the pan juices and pour them into a saucepan. Add the vinegar and sherry and cook over medium-high heat until the liquid is reduced by a third. Carve the chicken and pour the sauce over the pieces and serve.

S E R V E S 6 T O 8

Rock Cornish Game Hens with Szechwan Pepper Sauce

One of the beauties of Cornish game hens is that one whole bird is usually just about right to serve per person. Like most poultry, their mildly flavored meat makes them eminently adaptable to many different spicing treatments.

This recipe is quite spicy, in the Szechwan tradition, so it wouldn't hurt to put some beer on ice before you start cooking. Ice cold beer seems to go very well with spicy Chinese-style dishes.

2 Rock Cornish game hens
2 tablespoons Sesame Oil with Szechwan Peppercorns (page 23)
2 tablespoons Ginger Garlic Vinegar (page 29)
½ cup Szechwan Sherry (page 43)
1 tablespoon Szechwan peppercorns, crushed
1 teaspoon salt

Preheat the oven to 425°F. Wash the hens and dry them thoroughly. With a heavy sharp knife, cut down each side of the backbone of each hen. Reserve the backbone for another use or discard. Place the hens on a flat surface, back side down, and with your fist pound the breast bone to flatten.

With a sharp knife, make a small slit in the skin between the thigh and drumstick on each side of each hen. Tuck the end of each drumstick into the slit to secure it. Place the hens in a roasting pan, skin side down.

Mix the oil, vinegar, sherry, peppercorns, and salt. Baste the hens with the sauce and put them in the oven and roast for 20 minutes. Reduce the oven temperature to 350°F.

Turn the hens skin side up. Baste with the sauce and roast until the juices run clear when pierced with a knife in the thickest part of the thigh, about 30 minutes.

Reduce the remaining sauce in a small skillet over high heat until it is thick enough to coat the back of a spoon. Brush the hens with the glaze and put them under a broiler until they glaze over, 1 to 2 minutes. Serve immediately.

S E R V E S   2

Thai-style Chicken with Peanut Curry

This is a delicious dish that is easy and quick to prepare. It is quite spicy so make sure you have plenty of jasmine rice (available in Asian groceries) and ice cold beer to go along with it.

½ cup chunky-style peanut butter
1 teaspoon minced garlic
1 teaspoon freshly grated ginger
1 teaspoon hot curry powder
1 teaspoon crushed dried red pepper
1 teaspoon soy sauce
1 teaspoon fish sauce (available in Asian groceries)
1 teaspoon Curry Oil (page 20)
2 teaspoons Sesame Oil with Szechwan Peppercorns (page 23)
½ cup chicken broth
2 tablespoons peanut oil
2 whole boneless, skinless chicken breasts cut into thin strips
1 large sweet onion, peeled and cut vertically into strips
1 teaspoon minced lemon grass

In a mixing bowl combine the peanut butter, garlic, ginger, curry powder, chili pepper, soy sauce, fish sauce, and oils. Heat the chicken broth and pour it into the bowl and mix well.

Heat the peanut oil in a wok over high heat. When the oil is almost smoking add the chicken, onion, and lemon grass. Stir-fry until the chicken is cooked through, 3 to 4 minutes. Add the peanut mixture to the wok, stir to coat, and serve.

SERVES 4

Caribbean-style Grilled Chicken

The Scotch bonnet pepper, or its close relative the habanero, is native to the Caribbean. It figures prominently in Caribbean cookery and also enjoys the privileged status of being the hottest commercially cultivated pepper in the world. The interesting thing about these chilies is that in addition to heat, they have a distinctive flavor that adds to whatever recipe in which they are used.

4 scallions, cut into 1-inch pieces
2 Scotch bonnet or habanero peppers
⅓ cup lime juice
2 tablespoons Lemon Thyme Oil (page 22)
2 teaspoons dried thyme
1 teaspoon freshly ground black pepper
½ teaspoon salt
½ teaspoon ground cinnamon
½ teaspoon ground nutmeg
½ teaspoon ground allspice
2 whole boneless, skinless chicken breasts, about 1½ pounds, halved
6 cups mixed salad greens, such as leaf lettuce, bib, or romaine

1 cup bean or radish sprouts
1 small red onion, peeled, thinly sliced, and separated into rings
2 tablespoons lime juice
1 tablespoon Ground Hot Pepper Vinegar (page 29)
2 teaspoons sugar
⅓ cup Allspice and Bay Oil (page 17)

Combine the scallions, peppers, lime juice, oil, thyme, pepper, salt, cinnamon, nutmeg, and allspice in a food processor and process until everything is thoroughly blended. Place the chicken breasts in a shallow baking dish and pour the spice mixture over them. Turn the breasts to coat the spices evenly on both sides. Cover and refrigerate for 2 to 3 hours.

Prepare a charcoal fire or preheat a gas grill. Meanwhile, tear the greens into bite-sized pieces and divide them evenly among four serving plates. Do the same for the sprouts and red onion. Whisk the lime juice, vinegar, sugar, and oil together and set it aside.

Grill the chicken until it just done through and slightly charred on both sides, about 15 to 20 minutes. When the chicken is done, place it on a cutting board and slice it across the grain into strips. Divide the strips among the four plates, drizzle a little of the lime juice sauce on each, and serve. To be totally authentic, pass a bottle of habanero hot sauce at the table.

SERVES 4

Ginger Lime Chicken

This recipe uses classic flavor combinations, ginger and lime, that results in a piquant dish suitable even for company.

4 whole boneless, skinless chicken breasts, about 1½ pounds, cut into 1-inch chunks
2 tablespoons Ginger Garlic Vinegar (page 29)
2 tablespoons Lemon Mint Vinegar (page 31)
¼ cup lime juice
2 tablespoons Lemon Thyme Oil (page 22)
2 tablespoons soy sauce
2 tablespoons honey
2 tablespoons freshly grated ginger
2 tablespoons finely minced garlic
1 teaspoon crushed dried red pepper or to taste
1 teaspoon freshly ground black pepper
2 tablespoons minced cilantro (fresh coriander)
2 teaspoons cornstarch

Place the chicken pieces in a shallow baking dish. Combine the vinegars, lime juice, oil, soy sauce, honey, ginger, garlic, and red and black pepper. Pour over the chicken and marinate several hours or overnight, covered and refrigerated.

Thread an equal number of chicken pieces on metal or wooden skewers. (If using wooden skewers be sure to soak them in water for about 1 hour before using them.) Reserve the marinade. Prepare a charcoal fire or preheat a gas grill. When the fire is ready, cook the chicken over medium-high heat, turning once or twice, until the chicken is cooked through, about 10 to 12 minutes.

While the chicken is cooking, stir the cilantro and cornstarch into the reserved marinade. Cook the marinade in a saucepan over medium-high heat until it is thickened and slightly reduced. When the chicken is done place it on a serving platter, pour the marinade over, and serve.

SERVES 4

Chicken Spiedies

Every cuisine has its own version of the shish kabob. Simply put, spiedies are marinated pieces of meat (originally lamb), skewered and grilled over a charcoal fire. The word *spiedi* is probably a form of the Italian word *spiedini*, referring to something skewered.

1 pound boneless, skinless chicken breast, cut into 1- to 1½-inch pieces
¾ cup Lemon Mint Vinegar (page 31)
¼ cup freshly squeezed lemon juice
½ cup Lemon Thyme Oil (page 22)
1 teaspoon minced garlic
1 teaspoon dried oregano or 2 teaspoons minced fresh
1 teaspoon dried basil or 2 teaspoons minced fresh
1 teaspoon dried mint or 2 teaspoons minced fresh
1 teaspoon dried thyme or 2 teaspoons minced fresh
1 teaspoon salt
1 teaspoon freshly ground black pepper
½ teaspoon crushed dried red pepper

Place the meat in a baking dish and add the remaining ingredients. The longer the meat marinates, up to 2 or 3 days, the better the flavor.

Thread as many pieces (usually 4 or 5) of meat as will fit on a slice of Italian bread on metal skewers. Discard the marinade. Prepare a charcoal fire and grill the spiedies until the meat is lightly charred on the out-

side and no longer pink inside, 6 to 10 minutes. When the spiedies are done they are traditionally served by sticking a slice of Italian bread on each skewer and handing it to each diner. The diner then takes off the bread and wraps it around the pieces of meat and pulls them off the skewer.

Some spiedie aficionados insist on mixing up an extra batch of marinade (do not use the marinade used for the chicken), possibly adding 1 teaspoon or so of sugar, and spritzing the spiedies with this just before serving.

SERVES 4

Yakitori

Yakitori are pieces of skewered, marinated chicken, grilled over charcoal. They are a favorite in Japan, and if you try this recipe they're sure to become a favorite of yours.

4 chicken thighs, approximately 1 pound, skinned, boned, and cut into 1- to 1½-inch pieces
½ cup soy sauce
¼ cup Ginger Garlic Sherry (page 39)
1 teaspoon finely minced garlic
1 teaspoon freshly grated ginger
2 tablespoons Allspice and Bay Oil (page 17)
1 red bell pepper, cored, seeded, and cut into 1-inch pieces
4 scallions, trimmed and each cut into 4 pieces, white part only

Place the chicken in a shallow baking dish and add the soy sauce, sherry, garlic, ginger, and oil. Marinate, covered, several hours or overnight.

Chicken Spiedies

Soak four bamboo skewers for ½ hour. Thread the chicken, bell pepper, and scallions, alternating each, onto the skewers. Prepare a charcoal fire or preheat a gas grill. Grill the yakitori over medium-hot coals until the meat is no longer pink in the center, about 8 to 10 minutes.

SERVES 4

Chicken with Forty Cloves of Garlic

I suppose most people would think that forty cloves of garlic in any recipe is overkill. The fact is, as this classic French recipe proves, forty cloves can be just right. As pungent as raw garlic can be, when it is slowly roasted it loses its pungency and takes on an almost sweet, nutty flavor. Be sure to have some crusty French bread on hand. Diners should squeeze the garlic out of its skins onto the bread. After roasting the garlic is soft and spreads like butter.

2 tablespoons Provençal Oil (page 22)
1 whole frying chicken, about 3 to 3½ pounds, cut into 8 pieces
40 cloves (approximately) garlic, about 4 heads, separated but unpeeled
1 cup Lemon Mint Sherry (page 41)
1 cup chicken stock
1 teaspoon dried thyme
1 teaspoon rosemary, crushed
1 teaspoon dried marjoram
Salt and freshly ground black pepper
¼ cup brandy, warmed
¼ cup chopped fresh parsley

Heat the oil in a Dutch oven and add the chicken in a single layer (you may need to cook the chicken in batches). Brown the chicken lightly on one side, about 5 to 6 minutes, turn and brown on the other side. Scatter the garlic cloves around the pieces of chicken and cook 2 to 3 minutes more to brown the garlic slightly. Add the sherry, stock, thyme, rosemary, marjoram, salt, and pepper. Cover and simmer over low heat for approximately 1 hour. Test the chicken for doneness by piercing the meaty part of a thigh. If the juice is clear the chicken is done.

Warm the brandy in a small saucepan and pour it over the chicken. Light the brandy with a match (be careful not to burn yourself), shaking the pan gently, until the flames are extinguished. Put the chicken on a serving platter and scatter the garlic cloves around it. Garnish the chicken with the parsley. Pass the cooking juices at the table.

SERVES 4 TO 6

Pesto-stuffed Chicken

This chicken isn't exactly stuffed, but rather the pesto is spread between the skin and the flesh. The skin acts as a tent that seals in the herbaceous flavors of sweet basil. This allows the flavors and aromas to penetrate the flesh in a way seasoning the outside of the skin never could.

Chicken with Forty Cloves of Garlic

One 5- to 7-pound roasting chicken
1 cup fresh basil leaves
2 cloves garlic
½ cup extra virgin olive oil
2 tablespoons pine nuts
½ cup freshly grated Pecorino Romano cheese
Salt and freshly ground black pepper
2 tablespoons Garlic Basil Vinegar (page 29)

Very carefully insert your hand under the skin at the neck of the chicken and pull it away from the flesh. Work your hand under the skin across both breasts and work your way down to the legs. You should be able to loosen the skin all the way to where the drumsticks meet the thighs.

Preheat the oven to 350°F. In a food processor combine the basil leaves, garlic, oil, pine nuts, and cheese. Process until smooth. Scoop up a small amount of pesto with your fingers and work it under the skin, starting as far back as possible by the legs and thighs. Repeat this process on both sides, making sure the flesh is coated all the way to the front of the breasts. Wipe your hands clean and smooth out the skin all the way around the bird. Sprinkle salt and pepper inside the bird's cavity. Brush the vinegar on the outside of the skin, tuck the wings underneath the bird, and tie the legs together. Sprinkle the outside lightly with salt and pepper.

Place the chicken on a roasting rack and roast, uncovered, for approximately 2 to 2¾ hours, depending on the size of the bird. Allow the bird to rest for 15 minutes before carving.

SERVES 6 TO 8

CHAPTER SEVEN

Grains and Pasta

Linguini with Four Mushrooms

Now that many different varieties of mushrooms are being cultivated and are widely available in grocery stores, people who would never dare eat a wild mushroom picked in the wild can experience the wonderful flavor and excitement that the more exotic varieties have to offer.

¼ *cup Red Pepper Olive Oil (page 23)*
¼ *cup minced shallots*
1 pound sliced wild mushrooms, including Italian brown mushrooms, such as portobello or porcini
1 teaspoon dried oregano
½ *teaspoon dried thyme leaves*
½ *teaspoon dried red pepper flakes or to taste*
¼ *cup dry vermouth*
Salt and freshly ground black pepper to taste
8 ounces linguini, cooked and drained
2 tablespoons fresh parsley, minced
Freshly grated Pecorino Romano cheese

Heat the oil in a skillet over medium heat and sauté the shallots until just crisp-tender,

Linguini with Four Mushrooms

about 2 minutes. Add the mushrooms to the skillet and sauté until they begin to give up their juice. Add the oregano, thyme, red pepper, vermouth, salt, and pepper. Sauté over medium-high heat until most of the liquid evaporates. Pour the mushroom sauce over the linguini, toss, sprinkle with the parsley, and serve. Pass the cheese at the table.

SERVES 4 AS A SIDE DISH OR 2 AS AN ENTRÉE

Perciatelli Escargots (Pasta with Snail Sauce)

Escargots are usually thought of as falling within the province of French cuisine. Classical French cooking, however, derives from Italian Renaissance kitchens, and this recipe weds the best of both culinary cultures. The traditional flavor of snail butter is in this recipe but it is a novel way of serving the little gastropods.

1 pound perciatelli

¼ cup clarified butter

¼ cup extra virgin olive oil

¼ cup chopped shallots

2 tablespoons minced garlic

8 ounces Italian brown mushrooms, such as portobello or porcini

2 tablespoons cornstarch

1 cup chicken or clam broth

1 cup dry vermouth

½ cup Lemon Mint Sherry (page 41)

1 cup milk

Three 7-ounce cans French snails, rinsed and drained (3 dozen snails)

Salt and freshly ground black pepper to taste

½ teaspoon cayenne pepper or to taste

1 cup freshly grated Pecorino Romano cheese

Bring a large pot of water to boil. Cook the pasta until al dente, drain, and keep warm on a serving platter.

Melt the butter in a skillet over medium heat and add the olive oil. Sauté the shallots and garlic until just crisp-tender, about 2 to 3 minutes. Add the mushrooms and sauté until they begin to give up their liquid, about 3 to 4 minutes. Mix the cornstarch with the stock and vermouth and pour into the skillet, stirring, over medium-high heat, until the mixture begins to thicken.

Add the sherry and milk, stirring. When the mixture bubbles, add the snails and simmer 3 to 4 minutes. Pour the sauce over the pasta and sprinkle the cheese over all. Pass additonal cheese at the table.

SERVES 4 TO 6

Tortellini Primavera

This dish is perfect as a luncheon entrée or as a side dish for dinner. Use the following recipe as starting point but be creative with whatever vegetables are fresh and in season.

1 pound fresh asparagus spears, cut into 1-inch pieces

⅓ cup plus 1 tablespoon extra virgin olive oil

1 small zucchini, cut into ½-inch cubes

1 medium-size white onion, chopped

1 each small green, yellow, and red bell peppers, cored, seeded, and cut into ½-inch dice

One 16-ounce package fresh or frozen cheese tortellini, cooked according to package directions and drained

¼ cup Rice Wine Vinegar with Garlic (page 33)

1 teaspoon Dijon-style mustard

1 teaspoon finely minced garlic

Salt and freshly ground black pepper to taste

¼ cup freshly grated Parmesan cheese

Microwave or steam the asparagus pieces until just crisp-tender. Freshen under cold running water, drain, and place in a large mixing bowl. Heat 1 tablespoon of the oil in a skillet or wok over medium heat and sauté the zucchini, onion, and peppers until just crisp-tender. Add the sautéed vegetables to the bowl with the asparagus, along with the cooked tortellini.

In a small mixing bowl combine the vinegar, mustard, garlic, salt, and pepper. Add the remaining ⅓ cup olive oil in a thin stream, stirring, until the oil is incorporated. Pour the mixture over the tortellini and vegetables. Add the Parmesan cheese, mix, and serve.

SERVES 4 TO 6 AS AN ENTRÉE

Linguini with Sun-dried Tomatoes

Sun-dried tomatoes have gone from an esoteric specialty item in gourmet food shops to a staple on most grocers' shelves (albeit in the specialty foods department). Two basic type are available: those packed dry and those packed in olive oil.

1 pound linguini
¼ cup Pizza Oil (page 22)
¼ cup shredded fresh basil leaves
⅓ cup oil-packed sun-dried tomatoes, diced
1 teaspoon finely minced garlic
1 teaspoon crushed dried red pepper
Salt and freshly ground black pepper to taste
1 cup freshly grated Parmesan cheese

Bring a large pot of water to a boil and cook the linguini al dente. When the linguini is done, drain and keep it warm.

Heat the oil in the pot the pasta was cooked in over medium heat. Add the remaining ingredients except the cheese. Return the pasta to the pot, toss to coat evenly, and cook over low heat until warmed through. Put the pasta on a serving platter, sprinkle with 1 tablespoon of the cheese, and serve. Pass the remaining cheese at the table.

SERVES 6

Linguini with Basil and Pistachios

The aroma of sweet basil is intoxicating. It permeates the kitchen, saturates the air, and wafts up into your head like a magical elixir. A member of the mint family, the ancient Greeks called basil the royal herb, and for good reason. This dish marries the pungency of sweet basil with the delicate, subtle flavor of pistachios.

½ cup Fennel Oil (page 20)
1 tablespoon finely minced garlic
1 teaspoon freshly ground black pepper
1 teaspoon crushed dried red pepper
½ cup shelled pistachio nuts, coarsely chopped
1 cup whole basil leaves, shredded
Salt to taste
1 pound linguini, cooked al dente
1 cup freshly grated Asiago cheese

Heat the oil in a Dutch oven over medium heat. Add the garlic, black pepper, red pepper, and pistachio nuts. Sauté until the garlic just barely starts to brown, about 2 to 3 minutes. Add the basil leaves and salt. Add the linguini and toss, cooking over low heat, until the pasta is well coated and warmed through. Transfer the pasta to a serving platter, sprinkle with half the cheese, and pass the remaining cheese at the table.

SERVES 6

Fettuccine with Sun-dried Tomato Pesto

The traditional sweet basil pesto sauce has undergone countless permutations since it burst on the culinary scene a few years ago. No basil? Try parsley. No pine nuts? Try walnuts. This recipe is just another to add to your increasingly sophisticated pesto pantry of recipes.

1 cup oil-packed sun-dried tomatoes
½ cup freshly grated Parmesan cheese
½ cup freshly grated Pecorino Romano cheese
½ cup chopped walnuts
½ cup Pizza Oil (page 22)
Salt and freshly ground black pepper to taste
1 pound fettuccine

Place the sun-dried tomatoes in the bowl of a food processor and process coarsely. Add the cheeses and walnuts. Process until well blended. With the processor running, add the oil in a thin stream and process until the sauce is smooth.

Cook the fettuccine al dente, reserving about ¼ cup of the cooking water when draining the pasta. Mix the hot water with the pesto. Put the pasta in a serving bowl and toss with the pesto. Add salt and pepper to taste. Pass additional cheese at the table.

SERVES 6

Rigatoni with Sweet Red Pepper Puree and Sun–dried Tomatoes

Behind every green bell pepper is a sweet, ripe red pepper begging to be set free. Well, almost. It is true, however that the green masks the red pigment in a bell pepper. Every green pepper will turn red (or orange or yellow, depending on the species) when ripe. Red peppers are sweeter than their green cousins and are therefore perfectly suited to making a puree or sauce for dressing up some pasta.

2 large red bell peppers
¼ cup Pizza Oil (page 22)

1 small sweet onion, peeled and coarsely chopped
1 teaspoon minced garlic
½ teaspoon dried oregano or 2 teaspoons fresh, minced
½ teaspoon dried basil or 2 teaspoons fresh, minced
½ teaspoon dried thyme or 2 teaspoons fresh, minced
½ cup Allspice-flavored Sherry (page 37)
½ cup oil-packed sun-dried tomatoes, minced
Salt and freshly ground black pepper to taste
1 pound rigatoni or other tubular pasta

Roast the peppers. The easiest way to do this is to place them directly over a gas flame and char them on the outside all the way around. Or you can roast them in the broiler, turning occassionally. After the peppers are charred, place them in a paper bag, close the bag, and allow them to cool before proceeding. Peel the peppers (they should peel easily after having been roasted). Core, seed them, and coarsely chop them.

Heat the oil in a skillet over medium heat and add the onion and garlic. Sauté until the onion is soft, about 4 to 5 minutes. Add the peppers, oregano, basil, and thyme. Sauté 2 to 3 minutes. Puree the sauce in a blender or food processor until smooth. Return the sauce to the skillet and add the sherry and tomatoes. Heat through, stirring. Add salt and pepper to taste.

Cook the rigatoni al dente, drain and add to the skillet with the pepper puree. Toss to coat well, transfer the pasta to a serving platters, and serve.

SERVES 6

South of the Border Spaghetti

One of the great things about pasta is that it is so adaptable. This recipe includes some classic Tex-Mex elements to perk up your taste buds and wake up your appetite. The dish is best served at room temperature and the salsa can be prepared ahead of time, in which case simply don't sauce the pasta until you are ready to serve it.

1 pound spaghetti
One 28-ounce can whole tomatoes, coarsely chopped
4 to 5 jalapeño peppers, finely minced, including the seeds for a hotter salsa
2 to 3 serrano peppers, seeded and minced
1 small red onion, peeled and finely chopped
1 carrot, scraped and grated
2 tablespoons Chili Oil with Garlic (page 19)
2 tablespoons Ground Hot Pepper Vinegar (page 29)
1 teaspoon ground cumin
1 teaspoon dried oregano
1 tablespoon chili powder
1 teaspoon cayenne pepper
1 teaspoon salt
½ cup minced cilantro (fresh coriander)
1 cup shredded Monterey Jack cheese

Cook the pasta al dente, drain, rinse under cold water, drain thoroughly, and set aside.

In a mixing bowl combine the tomatoes, jalapeño and serrano peppers, onion, carrot, oil, vinegar, cumin, oregano, chili powder, cayenne pepper, and salt. Add the spaghetti to the bowl and toss to mix well. Transfer the spaghetti to a serving platter, garnish with the cilantro and pass with the cheese at the table.

SERVES 6 TO 8

Couscous

There are many different versions of this Middle Eastern staple. The basic ingredient is bulgur wheat. Bulgur wheat consists of wheat kernels that have been steamed, dried and crushed. In Morocco you're likely to encounter saffron in your couscous. Algerians are fond of tomatoes and in Tunisia the ingredient of choice is harissa, a fiery sauce made from chilies, garlic, coriander, cumin, and caraway.

FOR THE COUSCOUS:

1 ½ cups bulgur wheat (dry couscous)
½ teaspoon salt
1 ¼ cups boiling water
1 large red onion, chopped
2 carrots, diced and steamed until crisp-tender
1 sweet red bell pepper
1 cup peas (blanch fresh peas for 1 minute in boiling water or if using frozen thaw under cold running water since frozen peas are already blanched)
One 15-ounce can chick-peas, drained
½ cup Ginger Spice Oil (page 21)
¼ cup freshly squeezed lemon juice
½ teaspoon salt
½ teaspoon garlic powder
¼ teaspoon allspice
¼ teaspoon cayenne pepper
¼ cup minced fresh parsley
¼ cup minced fresh mint

FOR THE HARISSA:

½ cup Ginger Spice Oil (page 21)
¼ cup small dried red peppers
4 cloves garlic
1 teaspoon ground cumin
1 teaspoon ground coriander
1 teaspoon caraway seeds
½ teaspoon salt

Put the couscous in a bowl, add the salt and pour the boiling water over it. Let the couscous soak for about 30 minutes. Add the onion, carrots, red bell pepper, peas, and chick-peas. Mix through well.

In a mixing bowl combine the oil, lemon juice, salt, garlic powder, allspice, cayenne pepper, parsley, and mint. Mix well and pour this over the couscous. Allow this to sit for at least an hour to allow the flavors to blend.

Meanwhile, prepare the harissa. Pour the oil into a blender. With the motor running, add the remaining harissa ingredients, a small amount at a time, until everything is of puree consistency. Serve the couscous and pass the harissa at the table.

SERVES 4

Couscous

CHAPTER EIGHT

Vegetables

Paprika Potatoes

This classic dish is made all the more delicious by the addition of spicy chili pepper oil. Be sure to use sweet imported Hungarian paprika which has a depth of character that other paprikas lack.

1 pound russet potatoes, peeled or unpeeled,
  cut into ½-inch cubes
3 tablespoons butter or margarine
1 tablespoon Chili Pepper Oil (page 19)
1 medium-sized onion, diced (about 1 cup)
3 tablespoons sweet Hungarian paprika
2 teaspoons freshly ground black pepper
Salt to taste

Boil the potatoes in enough water to cover until they are cooked about halfway through (they will still be hard in the center when pierced with a fork), about 5 minutes. Drain and set aside. Heat the butter and the oil in a large, heavy skillet over medium heat and sauté the onion until it is crisp-tender, about 2 minutes. Stir the paprika into the onion. Add the potatoes and stir over medium heat until the potatoes are evenly coated with the paprika mixture. Cook, stirring, until the potatoes are cooked through, about 3 to 5 minutes. Add pepper and salt and serve.

SERVES 4

Pesto Mushrooms

Pesto pops up all over the place these days. This is an excellent side dish that is relatively easy to prepare and is simply delicious.

1 pound large white mushrooms suitable for
  stuffing
1 cup whole basil leaves
½ cup extra virgin olive oil
½ cup freshly grated Parmesan cheese
½ cup freshly grated Pecorino Romano
  cheese
¼ cup pine nuts
One 3-ounce package cream cheese
¼ cup mayonnaise
¼ cup freshly grated Parmesan cheese
¼ cup of the pesto you make with the above in-
  gredients
1 teaspoon Allspice-flavored Sherry (page
  37)

Dash hot pepper sauce, such as Tabasco
Freshly ground black pepper to taste

Remove the stems from the mushrooms and reserve for another use. Make the pesto by combining the basil, olive oil, cheeses, and pine nuts in a food processor and process until smooth. Combine the cream cheese, mayonnaise, Parmesan cheese, pesto, sherry, hot pepper sauce, and pepper. Fill each mushroom cap with an equal amount of stuffing. Serve chilled.

S E R V E S   6   T O   8

Stuffed Zucchini

Around about August when you get to the point where you simply cannot stand to look at another zucchini, try this recipe. It's guaranteed to wake up your taste buds and, yes, even let you look at another zuke without cringing.

2 small to medium zucchini
2 tablespoons Lemon Thyme Oil (page 22)
1 small onion, peeled and sliced
2 cloves garlic, minced
½ cup rice
½ cup Ginger and Red Pepper Sherry (page 39)
½ cup chicken stock
2 carrots, coarsely chopped
1 cup fresh or frozen sweet peas
¼ cup tomato paste
1 teaspoon dried thyme or 1 tablespoon minced fresh
1 teaspoon dried oregano or tablespoon minced fresh

1 teaspoon dried basil or 1 tablespoon minced fresh
Salt and freshly ground black pepper to taste

Preheat the oven to 375°F. Slice the zucchini in half lengthwise. Scoop out the seeds and flesh, leaving about ½ inch of flesh all the way around.

In a saucepan heat the oil over medium heat and sauté the onion and garlic for 2 to 3 minutes. Add the rice, stir to coat, and add the sherry and chicken stock. Bring to a boil, reduce the heat, cover, and simmer for 10 minutes. Add the remaining ingredients, cover, and simmer until the rice is tender, another 8 to 10 minutes.

Divide the stuffing equally among the four zucchini halves. Place the zucchini in a baking dish, pour about ½ cup of water around them, cover, and bake until the zucchini are tender, 40 to 45 minutes. Serve.

S E R V E S   4

Indian-style Potatoes and Cauliflower

In India this dish is known as *gobi aloo*. It's on the spicy side but you can control the heat by adding or subtracting the red pepper.

1 head cauliflower
¼ cup Chili Pepper Oil (page 19)
1 teaspoon crushed dried red pepper or to taste
1 teaspoon ground cumin
1 teaspoon turmeric
1 teaspoon ground coriander
4 large baking potatoes, cut into ½-inch cubes
½ cup water, approximately

Separate the cauliflower into individual florets. Heat the oil in a large skillet over medium heat and add the red pepper, cumin, turmeric, and coriander. Stir quickly and add the cauliflower and potatoes. Stir to coat the vegetables with the spices and oil. Add the water, cover, and cook over medium heat until the vegetables are tender.

SERVES 4

Ratatouille

Ratatouille is a classic from the Provence region of France. It's great summer food because it can be served hot or cold, is made from summer's bounty, and can be either an appetizer or main dish along with some crunchy French bread and a glass of red wine.

¼ cup Provençal Oil (page 22)
1 teaspoon minced garlic
1 large onion, peeled and coarsely chopped
1 medium-size eggplant, cut into ½-inch cubes
1 medium-size zucchini, cut into ½-inch cubes
1 green bell pepper, cored, seeded, and cut into ½-inch pieces
1 red bell pepper, cored, seeded, and cut into ½-inch pieces
1 teaspoon dried thyme
1 teaspoon dried basil
1 teaspoon crushed fennel seed
1 teaspoon dried marjoram
1 teaspoon summer savory
1 teaspoon crushed dried red pepper
One 28-ounce can whole plum tomatoes, broken into pieces, with their juice
Salt and freshly ground black pepper to taste

Ratatouille

Heat the oil in a large stockpot over medium heat and add the garlic, onion, eggplant, zucchini, and peppers. Sauté until the vegetables are just crisp-tender, about 5 to 6 minutes. Add the remaining ingredients, bring to a boil, reduce the heat, cover, and simmer gently until the vegetables are tender, 25 to 30 minutes. Serve hot or cold.

SERVES 4 AS A MAIN COURSE, UP TO 8 AS AN APPETIZER

Summer Stir-fry

This is a dish to make when summer's bounty is taking up every last square inch of your kitchen counter space. Feel free to substitute for any of the veggies here, depending on what your garden happens to be producing at the time.

2 tablespoons Sesame Oil with Szechwan Peppercorns (page 23)
1 teaspoon minced garlic
1 each red, green, and yellow or orange bell peppers, cored, seeded, and cut into strips
1 cucumber, peeled, seeded, and cut into ½-inch chunks
2 tomatoes, cored and cut into ½-inch chunks
1 small yellow squash, cut into ½-inch chunks
2 tablespoons Chinese chili paste with garlic (available in Asian groceries)
¼ cup Szechwan Sherry (page 43)
1 tablespoon cornstarch

Heat a wok and add the oil. When the oil is almost smoking add the garlic, peppers, cucumber, tomatoes, and squash. Stir-fry until the vegetables are just crisp-tender. Mix the sherry and cornstarch and add it to the wok. Stir-fry over medium-high heat until the sauce thickens and the vegetables are coated.

SERVES 4 TO 6 AS A SIDE DISH

Marinated Mushrooms

Plan on making these a day or two ahead of when you plan to serve them to give the marinade a chance to work its magic. Also, use only the freshest mushrooms.

½ cup Ginger Garlic Sherry (page 39)
2 tablespoons soy sauce
½ cup Rice Wine Vinegar with Garlic (page 33)
1 teaspoon crushed dried red pepper
1 teaspoon finely minced garlic
1 tablespoon finely minced shallots
5 to 6 whole black peppercorns
1 bay leaf
24 fresh mushrooms, stems detached and reserved for another use

Place all the ingredients except the mushrooms in a saucepan over high heat and bring to a boil. Reduce the heat and simmer 5 minutes. Put the mushroom caps in a mixing bowl and pour the liquid over them. Cover and refrigerate several hours or overnight before serving.

SERVES 4 TO 6

Baked Artichoke Hearts

This is a unique little side dish that doesn't take long to prepare and is surprisingly delicious considering how simple it is.

2 tablespoons Fennel Oil (page 20)
1 small onion, peeled and finely minced
Two 14-ounce cans artichoke hearts packed in water, drained
1½ cups mayonnaise
2 tablespoons Allspice-flavored Sherry (page 37)
1½ cups freshly grated Parmesan cheese
Salt and freshly ground black pepper to taste
½ cup toasted sliced almonds

Preheat the oven to 350°F. Heat the oil in a skillet over medium heat and sauté the onion until it is translucent, about 3 to 4 minutes. Transfer the onion to the bowl of a food processor and add the artichoke hearts. Process until the artichokes are coarsely chopped. Add the mayonnaise, sherry, and Parmesan and process until smooth. Add salt and pepper to taste.

Lightly grease a baking dish and scrape the mixture into it, then sprinkle the almond slices over the top. Bake until it is heated through, 15 to 20 minutes.

SERVES 4 TO 6

CHAPTER NINE

Fish and Seafood

Mahi Mahi Margarita

What margaritas do for our taste buds, they can also do for fish. Mahi mahi is becoming more common in fish markets these days. The flesh of mahi mahi is relatively firm and moderately fatty, which makes it a good candidate for grilling. This recipe adds a few nontraditional ingredients to your basic margarita. Also note that the original margarita recipe calls for lemon, not lime, juice.

4 mahi mahi filets or steaks, about 6 ounces
  each
1 cup gold tequila
¼ cup triple sec
1 tablespoon lemon juice
1 teaspoon minced garlic
1 serrano pepper, minced, with seeds
2 tablespoons Ginger Garlic Sherry (page 39)
¼ cup minced cilantro (fresh coriander)
1 teaspoon salt

Place the mahi mahi in a shallow baking dish. Add the tequila, triple sec, lemon juice, garlic, serrano, sherry, half the cilantro, and salt. Marinate, covered and refrigerated, turning once, for 1 hour. Drain and reserve the marinade.

Preheat a gas grill or prepare a charcoal fire. Grill the fish over medium heat until opaque, about 5 to 7 minutes. While the fish is grilling, pour the reserved marinade into a saucepan and cook, stirring, over medium-high heat until the liquid is reduced by half. Put the fillets on a serving platter, pour the sauce over, garnish with the remaining cilantro, and serve.

SERVES 4

Grilled Monkfish with Thai Vinaigrette

Monkfish goes by various aliases. It is sometimes called lotte, angler fish, sea devil, goosefish, and bellyfish. The only edible part of this fish is the tail, which closely resembles lobster meat in taste and texture. Because the meat of the monkfish is quite firm it is extremely versatile, taking to many different cooking techniques.

One 1-pound monkfish fillet

2 tablespoons Ginger Spice Oil (page 21)

¼ cup Rice Wine Vinegar with Lemon Grass and Kaffir Lime (page 33)

¼ cup Rice Wine Vinegar with Garlic (page 33)

½ cup Sesame Oil with Szechwan Peppercorns (page 23)

1 teaspoon fish sauce (available in Asian groceries)

1 teaspoon soy sauce

1 teaspoon finely minced garlic

1 Thai bird pepper, finely minced (available in Asian groceries)

2 teaspoons toasted sesame seeds

Place the monkfish in a shallow bowl. Combine the Ginger Spice Oil and the Rice Wine Vinegar with Lemon Grass and Kaffir Lime and pour it over the fish. Cover, refrigerate, and marinate for 1 to 2 hours.

Combine all the remaining ingredients and mix well. Prepare a charcoal fire or preheat a gas grill. Drain the monkfish and grill it over medium-hot coals, turning once, until the fish is cooked through, 10 to 12 minutes. Place the fish on a serving platter and slice it into ½-inch-thick slices. Pour the Thai vinaigrette over the slices and serve.

SERVES 4

Fillet of Salmon with Dill Vinegar Sauce

This an elegant dish to serve to company. It is relatively quick and easy to prepare and is delightfully delicious. Have your fishmonger skin and fillet the salmon for you. The sauce

Fillet of Salmon with Dill Vinegar Sauce

is simple to prepare and can be made ahead and refrigerated.

¼ cup sour cream

¼ cup plain low-fat yogurt

4 teaspoons Dill Oil (page 20)

1 tablespoon Tarragon Dill Vinegar (page 35)

½ teaspoon Tabasco sauce

1 tablespoon chopped fresh parsley

1 tablespoon chopped fresh dill

1 teaspoon chopped fresh tarragon

One 1½-pound salmon fillet

Salt and freshly ground black pepper to taste

Preheat the oven to 450°F. In a mixing bowl, combine the sour cream, yogurt, half the oil, the vinegar, Tabasco, parsley, dill, and tarragon. Beat or whisk to combine well.

Coat the bottom of a baking sheet with the remaining oil. Lay the salmon fillet on the baking sheet, sprinkle with salt and pepper and bake until the flesh is opaque, 10 to 12 minutes. Slice the fillet into serving-sized pieces and top with a dollop of the sauce.

SERVES 4 TO 6

Grilled Atlantic Salmon with Melon Salsa

Atlantic salmon, though not as plentiful as it once was, is still available at reasonable prices when in season, which is generally from early summer to early winter. Atlantic salmon has a high fat content and its flesh is deep pink and very succulent. The melon salsa cuts through the fat in the fish to provide the perfect counterpoint in taste and texture.

1 cup each of any 3 melons: honeydew, cran-
   shaw, cantaloupe, casaba, watermelon, or any
   other available varieties
½ cup diced red onion
1 red or green jalapeño pepper, cored, seeded,
   and minced
¼ cup minced cilantro (fresh coriander)
1 teaspoon ground cumin
¼ cup Lemon Mint Vinegar (page 31)
Four 6-ounce salmon steaks
¼ cup Lemon Mint Sherry (page 41)
2 tablespoons Lemon Thyme Oil (page 22)
1 teaspoon coarsely ground black pepper

Make the melon salsa by combining the melons, onion, jalapeño, cilantro, cumin, and
vinegar. Make the salsa several hours ahead
of time and refrigerate.

Place the salmon steaks in a shallow baking dish and pour the sherry, oil, and black
pepper over them. Turn to coat. Cover and
refrigerate 2 hours before proceeding.

Prepare a charcoal fire or preheat a gas
grill. Drain the salmon and grill over
medium-hot coals, turning once, until
cooked through, approximately 8 to 10 minutes. Spread ½ cup of salsa on each of four
dinner plates. Place a salmon steak on each.
Pass the remaining salsa at the table.

S E R V E S   4

Tex–Mex Grilled Salmon Steaks

Salmon is an excellent candidate for grilling
because it is a fatty fish that holds up well to
barbecue temperatures without drying out.

½ cup Ginger Garlic Sherry (page 39)
¼ cup orange juice
2 tablespoons lemon juice
1 teaspoon sugar
2 teaspoons finely minced garlic
2 teaspoons freshly grated ginger
1 teaspoon cayenne pepper
1 teaspoon ground cumin
¼ cup soy sauce
Four 4- to 6-ounce salmon steaks

Combine all ingredients except the salmon
steaks. Place the steaks in a shallow baking
pan and pour the marinade over them. Turn
to coat well. Refrigerate, covered, and allow
to marinate for about 1 hour.

Prepare a charcoal fire or preheat a gas
grill. Remove the salmon from the marinade
and reserve the marinade. Grill the steaks
over medium-hot coals, turning once about
halfway through the cooking time, about 10
to 12 minutes, depending on the thickness
of the steaks. Meanwhile, pour the reserved
marinade into a saucepan and cook over
medium-high heat until reduced by a third.
Pass the reduced sauce at the table with the
salmon.

S E R V E S   4

Swordfish with Hot Pepper Relish

This dish is not for those with a tender
palate. The habanero peppers provide the
heat kick of a mule. But they also have a flavor that marries well with the assertive flavor of swordfish. The moderately fatty flesh
of swordfish is firm and meaty. This recipe is
excellent whether broiled or grilled.

Swordfish with Hot Pepper Relish

1 red bell pepper, cored, seeded, and diced
1 green bell pepper, cored, seeded, and diced
1 small Vidalia onion, seeded and diced
2 habanero peppers, coarsely chopped
2 teaspoons minced cilantro (fresh coriander)
½ cup Rice Wine Vinegar with Garlic (page 33)
4 tablespoons Lemon Thyme Oil (page 22)
Four 6- to 8-ounce swordfish steaks
2 tablespoons lemon juice
Salt and freshly ground black pepper to taste

In a mixing bowl combine the peppers, onion, habanero, cilantro, vinegar, and 2 tablespoons of the lemon thyme oil. Set aside to allow the flavors to blend.

Place the swordfish steaks in a baking dish and coat with the remaining lemon thyme oil, lemon juice, salt, and pepper. Cover and refrigerate for about 1 hour.

Preheat the broiler or prepare a charcoal fire. Grill or broil the steaks 8 to 10 minutes, depending on thickness. Transfer the steaks to individual serving platters and spoon some of the relish over each. Pass the remaining relish at the table.

SERVES 4

Grilled Swordfish with Lemon–lime Sauce

Swordfish is simply wonderful grilled. It's fatty enough to stand up to heat and firm enough to make it easy to grill without worrying about it falling apart.

One 1-pound swordfish steak
1 cup Lemon Mint Sherry (page 41)
1 tablespoon Lemon Mint Vinegar (page 31)

1 tablespoon Rice Wine Vinegar with Lemon Grass and Kaffir Lime (page 33)
1 teaspoon freshly ground black pepper
Salt to taste
2 teaspoons cornstarch
1 tablespoon minced cilantro (fresh coriander)

Place the swordfish in a shallow baking pan. Combine the sherry, vinegars, pepper, and salt. Pour this over the swordfish and marinate, covered and refrigerated, for 1 to 2 hours.

Prepare a charcoal fire or preheat a gas grill. Remove the swordfish from the marinade and pour the marinade into a saucepan. Add the cornstarch to the marinade and cook over medium heat, stirring, until the sauce is thickened and slightly reduced.

Meanwhile, grill the swordfish over medium-hot coals until it is just done in the center, about 10 minutes. Serve and pass the sauce at the table.

SERVES 4

Grilled Swordfish with Black Beans and Garlic

Swordfish seems to have a natural affinity for the barbecue grill. Its firm, almost beeflike texture holds up well to the heat and smoke of a charcoal fire. This recipe combines some classic Chinese ingredients.

¼ cup Rice Wine Vinegar with Garlic (page 33)
1 teaspoon minced garlic
2 teaspoons freshly grated ginger
4 tablespoons Sesame Oil with Szechwan Peppercorns (page 23)

1 teaspoon freshly ground Szechwan pepper-
    corns
Four 6- to 8-ounce swordfish steaks
1 teaspoon minced garlic
¼ cup chopped scallions, white part only
    (finely mince the green parts and use as a
    garnish)
⅓ cup chicken stock
⅓ cup Ginger and Red Pepper Sherry (page 39)
⅓ cup Rice Wine Vinegar with Garlic (page
    33)
1 teaspoon soy sauce
1 tablespoon Chinese black beans with garlic
    sauce (available in Asian groceries)
1 tablespoon Szechwan hot bean paste (avail-
    able in Asian groceries)
1 tablespoon cornstarch

Combine the ¼ cup vinegar, garlic, 1 teaspoon of the ginger, 2 tablespoons of the oil,
and the peppercorns and pour it over the
swordfish. Turn the steaks to coat, cover, and
refrigerate for 1 to 2 hours.

Meanwhile, prepare the sauce. In a wok,
heat the remaining 2 tablespoons of oil over
high heat and add the garlic, remaining
1 teaspoon of ginger, and the scallions. Stir-
fry for 1 minute. Combine the chicken stock,
sherry, vinegar, soy sauce, black bean sauce,
bean paste, and cornstarch. Pour this mixture into the wok and stir-fry over medium
heat until the sauce thickens. Set aside and
keep warm.

Prepare a charcoal fire or preheat a gas
grill. Drain the swordfish and place over
medium-hot coals and cook approximately
3 to 5 minutes per side. Place the steaks on a
serving platter and pour a little bit of the

sauce over them and pass the remaining
sauce at the table.

SERVES 4

Grilled Rainbow Trout with Fresh Fruit Chutney

The chutney is a blend of seasonal summer
fruits with just enough of a kick to remind
you that you're not dining on fruit salad
here.

The easiest way to grill fresh rainbow
trout is in a fish grill basket. The fish is en-
tirely too tender to place directly on the grill
as it will fall apart before it's done. Grease
the basket before you place the fish in it and
they won't stick while cooking.

1 cup diced fresh peaches
1 cup fresh blueberries
1 cup whole fresh strawberries, halved
1 mango, peeled, pitted, and diced
1 cup fresh raspberries
1 small red onion, peeled and diced
2 tablespoons minced fresh mint leaves
Grated zest of 1 lemon
¼ cup Raspberry Lemon Vinegar (page 33)
1 small red chili pepper, minced
½ teaspoon allspice
½ teaspoon cinnamon
4 pan-dressed rainbow trout, about 8 ounces
    each
3 tablespoons Lemon Thyme Oil (page 22)
1 tablespoon lemon juice
Salt and freshly ground black pepper to taste

Combine all the ingredients listed before the
trout in a mixing bowl, cover, refrigerate,

and allow the chutney flavors to blend for several hours or overnight.

Prepare a charcoal fire or preheat a gas grill. Stuff each fish with as much chutney as will loosely fit in the cavity. Close the openings with toothpicks. Brush the fish with the oil and lemon juice. Sprinkle with salt and pepper.

Place the fish in a grill basket and grill over medium-hot coals until the fish just flakes with a fork, approximately 12 to 15 minutes. Do not overcook. Serve with the remaining chutney passed at the table.

S E R V E S 4

Grilled Salade Niçoise

A salade Niçoise is a classic combination of lettuce, tomatoes, sometimes potatoes, green beans, black olives, hard-boiled eggs, and tuna fish. Most commonly the tuna is from a can and packed in oil. This recipe adds a new twist in that the tuna is fresh. It is first marinated, then grilled.

½ cup Provençal Vinegar (page 31)
1 teaspoon finely minced garlic
1 teaspoon Dijon-style mustard
1 teaspoon freshly ground black pepper
½ teaspoon salt
¾ cup Provençal Oil (page 22)
One 1-pound fresh tuna steak
2 heads Boston bib lettuce
2 medium-size red potatoes, peeled, cooked, and sliced
½ pound green beans, blanched and chilled
2 ripe tomatoes, quartered
2 hard-boiled eggs, quartered
¼ cup oil- or brine-cured black olives

Combine the vinegar, garlic, mustard, pepper, salt, and oil. Place the tuna steak in a shallow baking dish and pour half the dressing over it. Turn to coat, cover, refrigerate, and marinate for about 2 hours.

Prepare a charcoal fire or preheat a gas grill. Grill the tuna steak until it is just barely rare in the center, about 6 to 8 minutes. Don't overcook it or it will dry out. When it is cooked, cut it into 1-inch pieces. Tear the lettuce into pieces and divide it among four salad plates. Divide the remaining ingredients among the four plates. Place an equal amount of the tuna pieces on each plate. Drizzle the remaining dressing over each salad and serve.

S E R V E S 4

Thai-style Clams with Chili Pepper Oil

If you like incendiary dishes this recipe will prove to be a real palate pleaser. In fact, there's enough fire in this recipe to win praises from any certified chili-head. Feel free to substitute fresh mussels for the clams. Either way, this dish is sure to fire up your taste buds as it sets your mouth on fire.

3 dozen fresh littleneck clams
1 tablespoon crushed dried red pepper
1 teaspoon freshly ground black pepper
2 tablespoons chopped cilantro (fresh coriander) roots
2 cloves garlic, finely minced
1 scallion, finely minced
2 tablespoons minced fresh lemon grass, bottom part only
4 to 5 Thai basil leaves, chopped

3 tablespoons Chili Pepper Oil (page 19)
¼ cup water
¼ cup minced cilantro (fresh coriander)

Scrub the clams and keep them chilled while preparing the chili paste. In a food processor, process the red pepper, black pepper, coriander roots, garlic, scallion, lemon grass, and basil. With the processor running, slowly add 1 tablespoon of the chili pepper oil. Scrape down the sides and process until it forms a smooth paste.

Heat a wok over high heat and add the remaining 2 tablespoons of chili pepper oil. Add the clams and shake or stir to coat the clams with the oil. Add the water to the wok and then the chili paste. Shake or stir to blend the water and chili paste. Cover the wok and cook over medium-high heat until the clams open, about 5 to 7 minutes. Discard any clams that fail to open. Garnish with the fresh cilantro and serve right from the wok. Plenty of ice cold beer and jasmine rice are the perfect accompaniments.

SERVES 4

Lobster with White Wine and Basil

Although lobster is generally best served simply steamed or boiled, this recipe makes the crustacean all the more special. It involves a little more preparation, but the results are worth it. This is definitely a company dish.

Four 1½-pound lobsters
2 tablespoons butter
¼ cup minced shallots
Pinch nutmeg
Pinch allspice
1 cup Five Spice Sherry (page 38)
1 cup clam juice
1 tablespoon cornstarch dissolved in 3 tablespoons water
¼ cup shredded fresh basil
Salt and freshly ground black pepper to taste
1 pound spaghettini, cooked al dente
¼ cup minced fresh parsley

Bring a large pot of water to a boil and cook the lobsters approximately 15 minutes, depending on their size. When the lobsters are done, remove them from the pot and when they are cool enough to handle, remove the meat from the tail and claws. Keep it warm. With a meat mallet crush the lobster shells into large pieces.

Heat the butter in a large skillet or wok over medium heat. Sauté the shallots until they are soft, about 4 to 5 minutes. Add the nutmeg and allspice and the broken lobster shells and sauté 5 to 6 minutes. Add the sherry and clam juice, bring to a boil, reduce the heat, and simmer gently for about 10 minutes. Strain the lobster stock through a sieve and return it to the skillet. Bring it to a boil and add the cornstarch mixture. Cook, stirring, over medium heat until the sauce thickens. Add the basil and season to taste with salt and pepper.

Divide the spaghettini among four dinner plates. Arrange the meat from one lobster on each plate in a decorative fashion. Pour an equal amount of sauce over each plate and serve.

SERVES 4

Scallops en Brochette

En brochette simply means "skewered." Because they tend to stick to things, one of the best ways to cook scallops is on a skewer. Recently some very large (under ten to a pound) sea scallops have been finding their way to market. They would be excellent in this recipe.

1 pound sea scallops
¼ cup Green Herb Oil (page 21)
¼ cup Ginger Garlic Sherry (page 39)
¼ cup orange juice
¼ cup Fines Herbes Vinegar (page 27)
2 teaspoons minced garlic
1 teaspoon freshly ground black pepper
¼ cup chopped fresh basil leaves
Salt to taste
3 lemons, thinly sliced

Place the scallops in a shallow baking dish. Mix the remaining ingredients except for the lemon slices and pour over the scallops. Marinate, covered and refrigerated, for 1 to 2 hours.

Thread the scallops on metal skewers, alternating scallops and lemon slices. Reserve the marinade. Preheat a gas grill or broiler. Grill or broil until the scallops are opaque, 4 to 5 minutes on each side. While the scallops are grilling, pour the reserved marinade into a saucepan and cook over high heat until reduced by half. When the scallops are done, place them on a serving platter, pour the sauce over, and serve.

SERVES 3 TO 4

Thai-style Shrimp with Tomatoes and Cucumbers

Although this dish can be incendiary, the combination of the tomatoes and cucumbers has a cooling effect that allows one to appreciate the flavor of the chilies as well as the heat. If you cannot find Thai basil and bird peppers in your local oriental market, feel free to substitute sweet basil and any hot green chili.

½ cup clam juice or fish stock
2 tablespoons soy sauce
1 ½ tablespoons cornstarch
2 tablespoons Chili Oil with Garlic (page 19)
1 cup coarsely chopped sweet onion
4 tablespoons chopped Thai bird peppers or other green chili peppers
2 tablespoons chopped garlic
1 stalk finely chopped lemon grass
¼ cup shredded Thai basil
6 kaffir lime leaves, shredded
¼ cup chopped cilantro (fresh coriander)
2 cups seedless cucumber, cut into ½-inch strips
2 cups diced fresh tomatoes, seeded and skinned, juice reserved
2 pounds jumbo shrimp, peeled and deveined, last tail segment left intact

Mix together the clam juice, soy sauce, cornstarch, and reserved tomato juice. Set aside.

Heat a large wok over high heat and add the oil. When the oil is almost smoking add the onions, bird peppers, garlic, lemon grass, all but 1 tablespoon of the basil, the lime leaves, and cilantro. Stir-fry over high heat 1 to 2 minutes. Add the cucumber and tomatoes. Stir-fry 2 to 3 minutes. Add the shrimp. Stir-fry until the shrimp are quite pink, 2 to 3 minutes. Add the cornstarch mixture and stir-fry until thickened, about 2 minutes. Sprinkle with the remaining tablespoon of oil and serve with plain or jasmine rice and ice cold beer.

SERVES 4 TO 6

Shrimp and Pesto Pizza

For some reason the flavors of shrimp and pesto seem a natural combination. If you're not into making pizza at home, you should definitely give it a try, especially after investing in a pizza stone. Pizza stones help your oven mimic the brick ovens of old by providing a porous surface on which to bake the pizza. This helps make for crisper crusts.

FOR THE PIZZA DOUGH:

1 tablespoon active dry yeast
¼ cup lukewarm water
4 cups bread flour
2 tablespoons Provençal or Thyme Oil (pages 22 or 23)
1 teaspoon salt

FOR THE TOPPING

1 cup pesto (page 126)
¼ cup each grated mozzarella, Asiago, Parmesan, and Pecorino Romano cheese
1 pound medium-size shrimp, peeled and deveined

To make the crust, dissolve the yeast in the water and allow it to start proofing, about 10 to 20 minutes. Put the flour in a mixing bowl. If using a mixer with dough hook, turn on the mixer and gradually pour the yeast into the bowl. If using your hands, make a well in the center of the flour, pour the yeast in, and begin mixing in the flour a little at a time until it is all incorporated. If using a mixer, add the oil and salt after the yeast. If using your hands, add the oil to the yeast liquid and sprinkle in the salt before mixing.

Regardless of the method used, knead the dough for several minutes to stretch the gluten. Divide the dough into two pieces, place each in a lightly greased bowl, cover, and allow to double in size. Punch the dough down, knead sightly, return it to the bowls, and let it double in size one more time before proceeding.

Preheat the oven to 450°F. Flour a nonstick cookie sheet. Pull and stetch one of the pieces of dough to form a circle on the cookie sheet about 14 to 16 inches in diameter. Spread half the pesto evenly on top of the dough. Sprinkle half the cheeses evenly over the pesto. Arrange half the shrimp on top of the cheese.

Slide the pizza off the cookie sheet onto the pizza stone and bake until the crust on the edges is brown and crisp and the cheese is bubbly, 10 to 15 minutes. Repeat the process for the other piece of dough.

SERVES 4 TO 6 AS A MAIN COURSE OR 10 TO 12 AS AN APPETIZER

Shrimp in Coconut Curry

The inspiration for this dish is definitely Thai in origin. What is so unique about Thai food is that it is as visually appealing as it is flavorfully complex. This particular dish relies on classic Thai curry ingredients which means that it rivals the heat from a four-alarm blaze.

4 to 5 cilantro roots
4 shallots, peeled
2 cloves garlic
6 to 8 Thai bird peppers (available in Asian groceries)
1 stalk lemon grass, bottom 2 inches only (available in Asian groceries)
1 teaspoon freshly grated ginger
2 teaspoons hot curry powder
One 16-ounce can coconut milk
¼ cup Bird Pepper Sherry (page 38)
1 pound large shrimp, peeled and deveined, last tail segment left intact
2 tablespoons minced cilantro (fresh coriander)

In a food processor (or with a mortar and pestle, if you want to be truly authentic), process the cilantro roots, shallots, garlic, bird peppers, lemon grass, ginger, and curry powder until it forms a paste.

In a wok, heat the coconut milk just to the boiling point. Add the sherry. Reduce the heat so it barely simmers and add the flavoring paste. Stir to blend well. Add the shrimp and continue to simmer until the shrimp are opaque and cooked through, 8 to 10 minutes. Sprinkle the minced cilantro over the shrimp and serve in bowls, preferably with jasmine rice.

SERVES 4

Shrimp Ravioli with Pesto

Ravioli are traditionally made from the same semolina dough from which all other pasta is made. By substituting wonton skins, you can make lighter ravioli that are not only easier on the stomach but can be filled with more delicate fillings. The pesto that dresses these shrimp-stuffed ravioli provides just the right foil for the slightly briny shrimp.

FOR THE RAVIOLI:

24 medium-size shrimp, peeled and deveined, shells reserved
1 tablespoon Thyme Oil (page 23)
¼ cup dry vermouth
1 teaspoon minced garlic
½ cup dry bread crumbs
2 tablespoons minced fresh basil
¼ cup minced oil-packed sun-dried tomatoes
1 egg, slightly beaten
Salt and freshly ground black pepper to taste
12 wonton wrappers
1 tablespoon cornstarch mixed with ¼ cup ice cold water

FOR THE PESTO:

2 cups firmly packed fresh basil leaves
¼ cup pine nuts
1 cup freshly grated Pecorino Romano cheese
½ cup extra virgin oil

Bring a pot of water to a boil and add the shrimp. When the water returns to a boil, turn off the heat and allow the shrimp to cook until they turn opaque, 2 to 3 minutes.

Drain the shrimp and chop them coarsely in a food processor.

Heat the oil in a skillet or wok. Add the reserved shrimp shells and vermouth and cook over medium-high heat until the shells turn pink and most of the vermouth is evaporated. Strain the shells though a sieve, pressing out as much liquid as possible back into the skillet.

Heat the remaining liquid and add the garlic. Sauté just until the garlic starts to turn soft. Turn off the heat and add the shrimp, bread crumbs, basil, tomatoes, egg, salt, and pepper. Mix thoroughly.

Arrange the wonton wrappers on a clean flat surface. Place equal amounts of the shrimp stuffing on each wonton. Brush the edges of the wrapper all the way around with the cornstarch mixture. Fold over the wrappers to form triangles. Press the edges to seal.

Steam the ravioli in a single layer in a vegetable steamer for 5 to 6 minutes. Turn off the heat and keep the ravioli warm.

Make the pesto sauce by combining the basil, pine nuts, and cheese in a food processor. While the processor is running, slowly add the oil until blended.

Place 2 tablespoons of pesto in the center of each of four serving plates. Spread the sauce to form a circle about 6 inches in diameter. Arrange three ravioli on each plate and top each with a small dollop of pesto.

SERVES 4

Baked Shrimp with Fresh Herbs

There is something special about the scent and flavor of fresh herbs. The aroma of fresh basil saturates the air around it with an unmistakable sweet pungency. Crush a few small oregano leaves between your fingers and you're almost transported to the south of Italy or a sunny Greek isle. The lemony, minty aroma of thyme leaves freshens the surrounding air. Fragrant, oniony chives bring to mind early spring when the days are warm and the nights are cool.

1 pound large shrimp, peeled and deveined
2 tablespoons Provençal Oil (page 22)
2 teaspoons minced garlic
1 tablespoon minced fresh thyme
1 tablespoon minced fresh basil
1 tablespoon minced fresh oregano
1 tablespoon minced fresh chives
2 tablespoons Lemon Mint Sherry (page 41)
1 teaspoon freshly ground black pepper

Preheat the oven to 425°F. In a mixing bowl combine the shrimp with all the other ingredients. Mix thoroughly to coat the shrimp well. Arrange the shrimp in a single layer in a baking dish and pour whatever liquid remains in the mixing bowl over them. Bake the shrimp until they are opaque and the oil is bubbling, 8 to 10 minutes.

SERVES 4 AS A MAIN COURSE OR 8 AS AN APPETIZER

Shrimp with Mango and Coconut Milk

The inspiration for this dish is somewhere between Indian and Thai cuisine. Like both cuisines, it is quite hot.

2 tablespoons Ginger Spice Oil (page 21)
1 large onion, diced
2 teaspoons minced garlic
2 teaspoons freshly grated ginger
4 to 5 Thai bird peppers, coarsely chopped (available in Asian groceries)
1 teaspoon ground coriander
1 teaspoon ground cumin
½ teaspoon turmeric
One 16-ounce can coconut milk
2 mangoes, peeled, pitted, and cut into chunks
1 pound large shrimp, peeled and deveined, last tail segment left intact
1 tablespoon minced cilantro (fresh coriander)

Heat the oil in a large skillet or wok over medium-high heat. Add the onion, garlic, ginger, and peppers and stir-fry over medium-high heat until the onion is just translucent, about 5 to 6 minutes. Add the coriander, cumin, and turmeric. Stir-fry 1 minute or so. Add the coconut milk and half the mangoes. Cook over medium heat until the liquid is reduced by half. Add the shrimp and remaining mango and cook, stirring, until the shrimp are cooked through, about 5 minutes. Garnish with the cilantro and serve.

SERVES 4

Ruth's Shrimp Fajitas

Although beef is the traditional ingredient in fajitas, chicken fajitas have become popular as people move away from eating red meat. This recipe takes the evolution of the fajita one step further and substitutes shrimp for the beef. The results are delicious! Thanks to my friend Ruth for coming up with the idea for this one.

1 pound large shrimp, peeled and deveined
¼ cup lime juice
¼ cup Lemon Thyme Oil (page 22)
2 tablespoons minced garlic
1 teaspoon crushed dried red pepper or to taste
2 tablespoons minced cilantro (fresh coriander)
4 soft flour tortillas
½ cup diced red onion
½ cup diced red bell pepper
¼ cup diced jalapeño peppers
½ cup shredded Monterey Jack cheese

FOR THE SALSA:

1 large, ripe tomato, cored and diced
¼ cup diced red onion
1 serrano pepper, seeded and diced
2 tablespoons minced cilantro (fresh coriander)
Salt to taste

Marinate the shrimp in the lime juice, oil, garlic, red pepper, and cilantro for about 2 hours, covered and refrigerated.

Wrap the tortilla shells in a damp dish towel and place them either in a warm oven or in a microwave on low power to warm them for 6 to 8 minutes.

Ruth's Shrimp Fajitas

Prepare a hot charcoal fire or preheat a gas grill. Drain the shrimp and grill them quickly over high heat. When they are opaque and slightly charred remove them to a serving platter. While the shrimp are grilling mix together the salsa ingredients. Place a warm tortilla on each of four serving plates and divide the shrimp evenly among the tortillas.

Allow each diner to assemble his own fajita by helping himself to the onions, bell pepper, jalapenos, cheese, and salsa.

SERVES 4

Hawaiian-style Sweet-and-Sour Shrimp

Julia Child, when once asked about shish kabobs, said to leave the vegetables in the salad bowl and put the meat on the skewer. As a corollary, I ordinarily believe in leaving the fruit in the fruit basket but every once in awhile an idea for a dish comes along that simply pleads for some fruit. This dish is simple, quick, and truly delicious. Prepare the batter ahead of time so that once you start cooking everything will move along quickly.

2 cups all-purpose flour
One 12-ounce bottle beer or ale
1 teaspoon freshly ground white pepper
½ cup Rice Wine Vinegar with Garlic (page 33)
1 tablespoon cornstarch
1 tablespoon soy sauce
½ cup chicken broth or clam juice
1 pound large shrimp, peeled and deveined, last tail segment left intact

1 cup peanut oil
1 green bell pepper, cored, seeded, and cut into 1-inch chunks
1 red bell pepper, cored, seeded, and cut into 1-inch chunks
2 large tomatoes, cored and seeded (squeeze as many seeds out with your fingers as you can)
1 cup fresh or canned pineapple chunks
2 tablespoons chopped cilantro (fresh coriander)

Prepare the beer batter by mixing the flour, beer, and pepper together in a medium-size bowl. Set aside for at least a couple hours to allow the alcohol to break down the gluten in the flour. (This is the secret to making a perfect beer batter.) Prepare the sauce by mixing the vinegar, cornstarch, soy sauce, and broth in a small bowl. Make sure the cornstarch is blended into the liquid without lumps. Add the shrimp to the beer batter and coat well.

Heat the oil in a wok over high heat. Remove a few shrimp from the batter, allowing extra batter to drip off. Cook the shrimp, a few at a time, until the batter is golden, about 3 to 4 minutes. As the shrimp are done, drain them on paper towels and keep them warm.

Drain off all but 2 tablespoons of the oil. Add the peppers, tomatoes, and pineapple to the wok and stir-fry over medium-high heat just until the peppers are crisp-tender, about 2 minutes. Return the shrimp to the wok and add the sauce. Stir-fry until the sauce thickens, about 1 to 2 minutes. Sprinkle the cilantro over all and serve with rice.

SERVES 4

Shrimp Fra Diavolo

This is a classic preparation for shrimp made even better with some of your homemade flavored oil and sherry. It's supposed to be spicy but use your own judgment with the chili pepper.

2 tablespoons Pizza Oil (page 22)
2 teaspoons minced garlic
1 small white onion, finely chopped
One 28-ounce can whole plum tomatoes
½ cup Jamaican Hot Pepper Sherry (page 41)
1 teaspoon dried thyme
1 teaspoon dried tarragon
1 teaspoon dried oregano
1 teaspoon freshly ground black pepper
Salt to taste
2 pounds large shrimp, peeled and deveined, last tail segment left intact

Heat the oil in a large skillet over medium heat and add the garlic and onion. Sauté until the onion is translucent, about 2 to 3 minutes. Break the tomatoes into pieces and add them with their juice to the skillet. Add the sherry, thyme, tarragon, oregano, and black pepper. Bring to a simmer and cook gently until the sauce is reduced by about a third, about 30 minutes. Taste and add salt according to your taste. Add the shrimp and simmer until the shrimp are opaque, about 5 to 7 minutes. Serve with pasta or rice.

Serves 6 to 8

Pesto Grilled Shrimp

Just when you thought there couldn't possibly be another way to enjoy pesto, surprise! Plan on marinating the shrimp for several hours to allow the sweet basil flavor to permeate the shrimp.

1 pound large shrimp, peeled and deveined, last tail segment left intact
¼ cup pesto (page 126)
¼ cup Provençal Oil (page 22)

Place the shrimp in a shallow baking dish and add the pesto and oil. Cover, refrigerate, and marinate several hours or overnight. Soak 4 bamboo skewers in water for at least 1 hour before threading the shrimp on them.

Prepare a charcoal fire or preheat a gas grill. Thread 4 to 5 shrimp on each skewer. Cook over medium-hot coals until the shrimp are opaque and cooked through, 5 to 6 minutes. Baste once or twice with the pesto oil.

Serves 4

CHAPTER TEN

Desserts

Jana's Raspberry Trifle

Decadent. Hedonistic. Sinful. Utterly delicious. Trifle. Practically every dessert cart in England is bound to have one version or another within its confines. This sponge cake, fruit, whipped cream, and custard dessert is usually well doused with sherry to warm the soul as it satiates the sweet tooth.

FOR THE CAKE:

4 eggs, separated
1 cup sugar
½ cup potato starch
1 teaspoon baking powder
Pinch salt

FOR THE CUSTARD FILLING:

3 eggs
2 tablespoons sugar
½ cup Vanilla Sherry (page 43)
1 cup milk
1 cup heavy cream

TO FINISH THE TRIFLE:

1 cup Vanilla Sherry (page 43)
2 cups fresh or frozen raspberries
1 cup raspberry preserves
1½ cups heavy cream
⅓ cup confectioners' sugar
1 teaspoon pure vanilla extract

Preheat oven to 350°F. Beat the egg whites until stiff. Beat the egg yolks and add the sugar, a little at a time, until it is incorporated. Sift together the potato starch, baking powder, and salt. Add the flour mixture to the egg mixture and fold well.

Grease and flour two 8-inch cake pans and divide the mixture between them. Bake for 20 to 25 minutes, or until done—a toothpick inserted in the center should come out clean. Allow the cake to cool on a wire rack before proceeding.

To make the custard filling, beat the eggs and mix in the sugar in the top half of a double boiler set over hot water. Heat the sherry, milk, and heavy cream in a saucepan over medium heat for 4 to 5 minutes. Gradually add this to the egg mixture, stirring constantly over low heat, until the mixture thickens and coats the back of a spoon.

To finish the trifle, cut the cake into ½-inch slices. Line the bottom of a trifle bowl (or any large bowl) with one third of the slices. Sprinkle the cake slices with ⅓ cup of the sherry. Spread the raspberries over the cake. Spread one third of the custard over the raspberries.

Layer another third of the cake slices over the custard. Sprinkle the cake with ⅓ cup of the sherry. Spread the raspberry preserves over the cake. Spread another third of the custard over the raspberry preserves. Layer the remaining cake slices over the custard, sprinkle with the remaining sherry, and spread the remaining custard over the cake.

Beat the heavy cream until it forms peaks. Gently fold in the confectioners' sugar and add the vanilla extract. Spread the whipped cream over the top of the trifle. Refrigerate for 1 to 2 hours and before serving.

S E R V E S   1 0   T O   1 2

Summer Fruit Medley

When summer's bounty is threatening to overwhelm you with every imaginable sweet, fresh, plump fruit, and the sun's heat threatens to chase you out of the kitchen forever, why not give this recipe a whirl? It's easy, it uses whatever fresh fruit you have on hand, it's light, and it doesn't require but a minute of time at the stove. Feel free to substitute whatever fresh fruit you have for the ones in the recipe.

1 cup Lemon Mint Sherry (page 41)
1 cup Vanilla Sherry (page 43)
2 cups water
1 cup sugar
4 peaches, pitted and quartered
4 plums, pitted and quartered
4 nectarines, pitted and quartered
2 pears, cored and quartered
1 cup blueberries
1 cup blackberries

Heat the sherries and water over medium heat in a saucepan. Stir in the sugar and cook, stirring, until the sugar dissolves. Add the remaining ingredients and cook over medium-low heat for 8 to 10 minutes. Chill for at least 1 to 2 hours and serve.

S E R V E S   8

Tortoni

This is another slightly decadent dessert which makes the perfect coda to an Italian meal. Tortoni are as ubiquitous in Italy as trifle is in England. They are sometimes referred to as biscuit tortoni.

1 envelope unflavored gelatin
½ cup Vanilla Sherry (page 43), chilled
½ cup corn syrup
½ cup sugar
2 eggs
2 teaspoons pure vanilla extract
1 teaspoon almond extract
1½ cups heavy cream
¼ cup confectioners' sugar
¼ cup coarsely chopped toasted almonds
½ cup vanilla wafer crumbs

Dissolve the gelatin in the sherry. Heat the corn syrup in a saucepan over medium-low heat and add the sugar. Cook, stirring, until the sugar dissolves. Add this mixture to the gelatin. Beat the eggs and add the sugar syrup mixture. Stir in 1 teaspoon of the vanilla and the almond extract.

Beat the heavy cream until until soft peaks form. Fold in the confectioners' sugar. Add the remaining 1 teaspoon of vanilla. When the egg and sugar mixture is cool, add it to the whipped cream. Fold in the almonds and pour the mixture into paper muffin cups. Sprinkle vanilla wafer crumbs on top of each cup. Place the cups in the freezer until the tortoni are firm and serve.

SERVES 6 TO 8

Poached Pears

Sometimes the simplest desserts are the perfect finale. Furthermore, if you've overindulged in the calorie column during the rest of the meal, then something like these sherry-poached pears are just the ticket to assuage any pangs of guilt.

4 pears
Juice of 1 lemon
1 lemon, quartered
3 cups Lemon Mint Sherry (page 41)
2 tablespoons minced fresh mint

Core the pears from the bottom so as to leave the stem end intact, and peel them. Brush them with the lemon juice to prevent browning.

Put the lemon quarters in a saucepan, add the sherry, and bring the liquid to a boil over high heat. Add the pears upright, cover, reduce the heat, and simmer just until the pears are tender, approximately 15 minutes. Allow the pears to cool in the liquid.

Place the pears in individual serving dishes. Bring the poaching liquid to a boil and reduce by one third. Allow the liquid to cool to room temperature and then pour it over the pears. Garnish the pears with the fresh mint and serve.

SERVES 4

Zuccotto

Zuccotto is a classic Italian dessert from Tuscany. The story, which may very well be apocryphal, goes that the dessert was inspired by the dome of the main cathedral in Florence. There is a similarity in shape but regardless of where the idea for this confection came from, it's sinfully rich and delicious. Use the recipe for cake on page 132 or do as many Italians do and buy one.

½ cup hazelnuts
½ cup blanched almonds
2 cups heavy cream
½ cup confectioners' sugar
1 teaspoon pure vanilla extract
One 4-ounce piece bittersweet chocolate
One 16-ounce pound cake
2 tablespoons Vanilla Sherry (page 43)
2 tablespoons Cointreau or other orange-flavored liqueur
2 tablespoons light rum
2 tablespoons cocoa powder

Summer Fruit Medley

🌿 *A Dash of Elegance*

Preheat the oven to 425°F. Place the almonds and hazelnuts on a baking sheet and toast them in the oven for 4 to 5 minutes. Don't let them burn. Put the nuts in a food processor and coarsely chop them.

Whip the cream until it forms peaks and fold in the confectioners' sugar and vanilla extract. Grate the chocolate and fold it and the nuts into the cream.

Slice the pound cake into ½-inch-thick slices. Line a round bowl (a salad bowl is perfect for this) with either damp cheesecloth or buttered waxed paper. (Instead of buttering the waxed paper you can spray it with vegetable cooking spray.) Arrange slices of cake around the sides and bottom of the bowl, coming up to the rim. The slices should be touching each other all the way around.

Sprinkle the slices with a mixture of the sherry, Cointreau, and rum. Fold the whipped cream mixture into the bowl, smooth the top, and cover with the remaining cake slices. Sprinkle the remaining sherry, Cointreau, and rum over the cake.

The zuccotto is best refrigerated overnight before proceeding. To unmold the zuccotto invert a serving plate over it, turn it over, and tap it to release it from the bowl. The cheesecloth or waxed paper should come off easily. Dust the zuccotto with the cocoa and serve.

SERVES 6 TO 8

Poached Pears

Index

oil with fines herbes, 21
Provençal oil, 22
Provençal vinegar, 31–33
rice wine vinegar with shallots and, 34
see also specific herbs
honey:
    Dijon dressing, chicken salad with, 61–62
    gingered chicken, 93–94
hot-and-sour:
    soup with hot pepper sherry, 50–51
    vegetables, Cajun-style smoked sausage with, 76
Hunan-style meatballs, 81–82

Indian-style:
    lamb curry, 90
    potatoes and cauliflower, 111–13
ingredients, 15–16

jalapeño sherry, 39–41
Jamaican:
    hot pepper sherry, 41
    shrimp salad, 57
Japanese grilled beef, 67

kabobs:
    chicken spiedies, 97–99
    pork, with chili plum sauce, 74
    pork, with mango pineapple chili sauce, 74–75
    scallops en brochette, 124
    shrimp satay, 66–67
    yakitori, 99
keftas, lamb, 89–90
Korean-style beef (bulgogi), 83

lamb:
    curry, Indian-style, 90
    keftas, 89–90
    marinated leg of, 87–88
    patties, Middle Eastern, 88–89
    roast stuffed leg of, 88

lemon:
    broccoli soup, 50
    garlic chicken, roast, 94
    garlic vinegar, 29–31
    lime sauce, grilled swordfish with, 120
    mint sherry, 41
    mint vinegar, 31
    raspberry vinegar, 33
    thyme oil, 22
    veal, 79
lemon grass, 15, 16
    rice wine vinegar with kaffir lime and, 33–34
lime:
    ginger chicken, 96–97
    kaffir, rice wine vinegar with lemon grass and, 33–34
    lemon sauce, grilled swordfish with, 120
    and rose petal sherry, 41–43
    tequila sauce, grilled pork loin chops with, 70–71
linguini:
    with basil and pistachios, 105
    with four mushrooms, 103
    with sun-dried tomatoes, 105
lobster with white wine and basil, 123

malt vinegar, 5
mango:
    grilled pork chops with, 73–74
    pineapple chili sauce, pork kabobs with, 74–75
    shrimp with coconut milk and, 129
margarita:
    grilled pork loin chops with tequila lime sauce, 70–71
    mahi mahi, 115
meat, *see* beef; lamb; pork; veal
meatballs:
    Hunan-style, 81–82
    lamb keftas, 89–90
    Thai-style, in red curry, 67–68
Mediterranean-style tomato and onion salad, 57–58
melon salsa, grilled Atlantic salmon with, 117–18
Middle Eastern lamb patties, 88–89
mint:
    lemon sherry, 41
    lemon vinegar, 31